SMARTER Success offers you a method of creating success in each major area of your life. It will help you achieve and balance success in your:

- family
- career
- health
- finances
- relationships
- spiritual beliefs

SMARTER Success will not tell you what to think. It will simply offer information and ideas for your consideration.

SMARTER Success *will* require you to think, however. To attain smarter goals, you will have to think for yourself and on your own. You will need to make up your own mind. You will need to decide what it is you really want.

SMARTER Success is based on ancient information and is presented in a new way that offers you a fresh perspective on success. It contains ideas that have been handed down through the ages. Every generation throughout history has tested these ideas. The concepts are based on the philosophies of classic and modern, thinkers, teachers, preachers, orators, artists, doctors, scientists, business executives, comedians, politicians, and parents.

SMARTER Success describes how to create and control change. It is about getting what you want out of life without taking the life out of what you want. It is not about delaying gratification. It is about expediting satisfaction, pleasure, prosperity, and peace.

SMARTER Success is neither a manual that provides a formula for you to follow nor a map that will tell you precisely where to search for success. It will not reveal a shortcut, but it will show you a smarter path that will enable you to fulfill your desires while you are pursuing your own dreams of the future.

SMARTER Success describes a technique for setting goals that works like a compass and keeps you headed in the right direction. The ideas are not so much about reaching a destination as they are about traveling on the right path.

SMARTER Success will help you realize that there are at least two types of goals you can set in your life. You can join the race to *have* something, or you can strive to *be* something. One type of goal can help you *have* more and the other can help you *be* more.

SMARTER Success is about becoming rich beyond expectation. It offers you ways of measuring your own success with means other than numbers on a financial statement. When you fully realize your potential and appreciate the natural splendor that surrounds you, immeasurable wealth will be yours.

SMARTER Success will offer you the keys to success. Actually, you don't need a key to attain success. It may take work to open the door to success, but the door is not locked. The door to happiness and prosperity swings freely when you stop trying to push it open. With a gentle pull, the door to success opens inward to allow your inner potential to be expressed.

SMARTER Success will disclose the secrets of success. However, there really are no secrets. The information in this book is not clandestine or private; it is all within the public domain. If there is any secret to success, it is found in understanding ideas and concepts that have been with us forever. . This book explains wisdom of antiquity that might be unfamiliar and reveals knowledge that makes it possible for anyone and everyone to be successful.

SMARTER Success is not about finding an easy way to reach your destination. Worthy goals require work. It is about working smarter along the way. Easy, difficult, and hard become meaningless descriptions of a task when you enthusiastically enjoy what you are doing.

SMARTER Success will offer you ways to attain success for yourself, in your own way, at your own pace.

S.M.A.R.T.E.R.
success

S.M.A.R.T.E.R.
success

How to find your path to peace and
prosperity by using S.M.A.R.T.E.R. goals

Dr. Al Lippart

MVC Productions
Green Lake County, WI

Published by MVC Productions
P.O. Box 614
Markesan, WI 53946

Publisher's Cataloging-in-Publication Data
Lippart, Al.
    SMARTER success: how to find your path to peace and prosperity by using SMARTER
    goals / Al Lippart, Sarah Riley--Markesan, WI : MVC Productions, 2003.

        240 p. : 23 cm.
        ISBN: 0-9713109-0-4

        1. Success. 2. Goal (Psychologoy). 3.Self-realization. 4. Self-actualization
        (Psychology). I. Riley, Sarh. II. Title.

BF637.S8 L57 2003   2001118529
158.1--dc21   0307

Book coordination by Nikki Stahl of Jenkins Group, Inc. • www.bookpublishing.com
Cover design by Kelli Leader
Interior design coordination by Leah Nicholson
Interior design by Debbie Sidman/Paw Print Media
Interior illustrations by Sarah Riley, age 12

Books published by MVC Productions are available at quantity discounts on bulk purchases for premium, educational, fund-raising, and special sales use. For details and requests, please e-mail: sales@lippart.com.

Cover photo by John R. Hartman, Contemporary Photography, 1416 Clark Street, Stevens Point, WI 54481

Printed in the United States of America
07 06 05 04 03 • 5 4 3 2 1

Prologue

I have cared for animals who have returned unconditional love. I have
worked with people who loved and cared for animals and displayed
kindness beyond expectation. I have helped to develop the potential of
four children, two sons and two daughters, and it has given me great satisfaction to see them become well-adjusted adults. I have shared my life with a
loving wife. I have dreamed and watched dreams become reality through the
power of faith. Because of these experiences, I have known the greatest
wealth. In this book, I share my abundance with you.

Contents

Acknowledgments

*T*he history of *SMARTER Success* began many years ago when a few significant situations serendipitously fell into place. First, my parents, Roy and Edna, let me have a pony. Princess was my first pet and she taught me a lot about the facts of life. On one particular Friday, my grandfather told me I was feeding her too much; she was getting too fat. The next Monday when I went out to take care of her, she had a foal by her side. Without knowing it at the time, Mom and Dad had provided me with a pregnant pony, my first animal husbandry project. My folks also allowed me to raise white rats, physically challenged cats, a horse, skunks, and several dogs. Their guidance and tolerance were essential elements in the development of my career and this book.

About the time I was fifteen and needed a job after school, Dr. Paul Didion and Dr. Jeff Hamann decided to build a new veterinary clinic. They needed help moving all of their medicines and supplies to the new facility. It became my job to haul boxes, build and stock shelves, install towel holders, clean kennels, and assist the doctors however I could. As I learned and matured, I was given more responsibilities in the clinic and on farm visits. The veterinarians were crucial characters in the progression of my education and they became the basis upon which my character and career were built. Their integrity, honesty, and morality are attributes I attempt to emulate to this day.

The direction I received from Robert Flegl and Kay Schulze were fundamental factors in my intellectual development. They inspired me to contemplate concepts and to cogitate convictions that I had always held as solid facts. With their tutelage I began thinking about questions regarding elementary dogma and metaphysical minutia that intrigue me yet today.

Before my ideas were put into print, they were tested with my own family and friends. I owe a debt of gratitude to: my wife, Kerstin; children, Christopher, Michelle, Paul, and Sasha; dog, Linie; the staff of the Markesan Veterinary Clinic, especially Carie Schmitz, Pamela Draheim, and Joy Weigel; friends and assistants along the way, Becky Buehl, Rebecca Reichert, Libby Glenn, Judy Paulsen, and Sue Johnson; the Jenkins Group, especially Nikki Stahl, Kelli Leader, Mareesa Orth, Leah Nicholson, editor Carol Cartaino and designer Debbie Sidman; artist Sarah Riley, age 12; and all of the clients and animals with whom I have interacted through the last half century. It has been a privilege to work with you and to enjoy our time together. Collectively, you have helped me create *SMARTER Success* as a book…and a way of life.

 *Foreword by Linie*

Linie, pictured with the author in the cover photo, is a female Golden Retriever. Her name is Norwegian and is pronounced Lē nē ă.

For years, I have been encouraging Dr. Lippart to write a book about success and animals. Perhaps he didn't listen or maybe he just didn't understand me. Now, at last, he has taken my advice. With my help and inspiration, he has created this book in which he shares with you what he learned from me.

Like many humans I have met, Dr. Lippart has worked diligently to create a career and family. I have found him to be a good student, also. While in college, he learned about animal anatomy, medicine, and surgery. I, along with many of my animal colleagues including cats, cows, and horses, taught him everything else he knows. We have shown him natural sources of success and happiness. He has compiled what he has learned and now shares our ideas with you in this book that can help you find success for yourself.

Animals, especially dogs like me, can offer humans a great deal of insight into life. From us you can learn to find enjoyment in simple things like taking a nap, going on a long walk, and feeling the fresh air and wind in your face. Also, we can teach you about:

Happiness   When you're happy, I suggest you dance around and wiggle your entire body.

Nutrition   Select a healthful diet and then eat with enthusiasm. Stop when you have had enough.

Exercise	Remember to stretch your muscles and then exercise them regularly by jogging and playing. Chase imaginary rabbits around the yard if you don't have a friend to play with. People might think you are goofy, but don't let that stop you. Exercising or moving around when you get stressed out can help eliminate the need for caffeine, alcohol, and anti-depressants.
Relationships	Add zest to your relationships by running to greet loved ones when you meet. Don't bore people with your troubles and resist complaining. I never do. When others are having a bad day, be quiet, sit close, and nuzzle them gently. My kitty colleagues suggest you purr, if you can.
Self-esteem	Accept criticism and blame even if you know you are not responsible, but don't let it bother you. When you are unjustly accused, just act like you have no idea what happened or why.
Love	Give love unconditionally to those you care about.

SMARTER Success is a serious book about a very important subject—your health and happiness. But that doesn't mean it is without humor. It is important to laugh and smile whenever you can. Feel free to do so whether you think the author is funny or crazy. You may not agree with some of his ideas, but please think about them. Contemplation and consideration are cornerstones of voluntary change.

Some of Dr. Al's advice is simple wisdom that he has supported in this book with quotes from over one hundred humans. *SMARTER Success* offers a unique technique that can help you find your path to peace and prosperity while balancing your emotions and relationships and maintaining your natural health and happiness. Be ready to change your mind about things you thought you understood.

Animals offer simple answers to life's most serious questions. When you decide what is really important to you, the ideas in this book will help you find your path. If your path is not obvious at first, it's because society has covered it with materialistic ideals, which are meaningless to other animals.

I hope you find what you are looking for. Some of the answers you seek are deep. Start digging and don't stop until you find your heart's desire. 🐾

Somewhere along the way

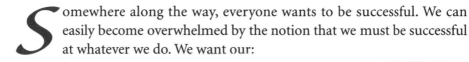

Somewhere along the way, everyone wants to be successful. We can easily become overwhelmed by the notion that we must be successful at whatever we do. We want our:

…lives to be successful.
…careers and occupations to be successful.
…marriages and families to be successful.
…children to be successful.
…financial investments to be successful.
…schools to be successful.
…sports teams to be successful.
…favorite political candidates to be successful.
…military forces to be successful.
…doctors to be successful in finding out what ails us.
…surgeons to be successful when our bodies require operations.
…pharmaceutical companies to be successful in developing new drugs.
…spiritual lives to be successful.

Somewhere along the way, we feel pressure from others who expect us to be successful.

- Parents expect us to grow up and become successful individuals.
- Children expect us to raise and care for them successfully.
- Teachers expect us to learn successfully.
- Employers expect us to perform successfully at work.
- Clients expect us to meet their expectations successfully.
- Customers expect us to serve their needs successfully.
- Peers expect us to compete for success.

Somewhere along the way, we learn that to be successful we need to have money, power, and property.

Somewhere along the way, we learn that the more "stuff" we collect the more successful we are.

> *Rich or poor, we all collect material possessions that seem useful or important at one time or another. When the things we gather become too numerous to count or list, they become nondescript "stuff."*

Advertisements in newspapers, magazines, movies, and music bombard us with incentives to buy things that will make us look, smell, or feel successful. Commercials on television, radio, billboards, and storefronts tell us how we can become successful by purchasing and using the sponsors' products. Everyone has something to sell us that will make us successful.

A better suit will make an executive look successful.

A designer name on a shirt will create a successful image.

A logo on athletic shoes will help a team have a successful season.

The right clothes, cosmetics, and smell will ensure a successful love life.

> The right fragrance will attract a mate.
>
> Makeup will create an attractive face and body.
>
> Hair coloring will change our appearance and make us look younger.
>
> Undergarments and seductive outfits will enhance our sex appeal.

The right car will make us feel and look successful.

> SUV's will make us appear to be the rugged outdoors type.
>
> A sporty car will make us appear younger.

A large elegant car will make us appear wealthy and at the top of
our field.

An expensive car will let people know we have made it in a big way.

Much of the American economy is based upon the sales of things that
will make us feel, smell, look, and sound successful. Marketing has made
shopping the number one pastime of many Americans. If we only
had enough money, we could all be successful—or at least appear as
though we were.

Somewhere along the way, we learn that if we want to have something, we
can make it our goal to get it.

Somewhere along the way, we learn that if we work hard enough and work
smart enough, we can have anything we want.

If a goal is specific, measurable, acceptable, and realistic, we can get anything we want in a limited amount of time.

However...

Somewhere along the way, we forget the real reasons behind our desires to
reach goals.

Somewhere along the way, we forget that success does not always create
happiness.

Somewhere along the way, we forget that we will never *have* happiness
unless we learn to *be* happy while pursuing our goals.

Somewhere along the way, we need to take our eyes off of our destination
and look closely at the path beneath our feet.

Somewhere along the way, we need to stop and realize that success and
happiness are not destinations toward which we must work. We simply need
to be happy while we work, play, and live.

Somewhere along the way, we need to slow down and ask ourselves a few
important questions. Are we happy most of the time? Is there anything we
can do to make life better? Are the
plans we made in the past still
appropriate today? Are we still on
the right path? Where are we
really headed? Should we set new
goals? If we set goals, how do we
do it? What kind of goals do we
set? What is it that we really want?

> *We know that goals help us
> get where we want to go.
> The challenge is to know where it is
> we are going.* ❧

The answers to these questions are most meaningful and appropriate when they come from your own thinking. In the end, only your own answers are significant and relevant. No one should tell you what to think or force answers upon you. However, learning how others have dealt with similar questions can help you formulate answers for yourself.

Somewhere along the way, we need to realize there are at least two basic ways to set a goal. We can set a goal to *have* something, or we can set a goal to *be* something. This concept is the most significant idea presented in this book.

> *There are two kinds of goals:*
>
> To **have** *something*
> To **be** *something*

Somewhere along the way, we assume that if we can *have* enough success, we can *be* happy. But this assumption is incorrect. Life doesn't work that way. Happiness doesn't come from having things. It comes from thinking happy thoughts. We must simply learn to *be* happy.

If we want to be happy and healthy, there is a smarter way to think about success. If we are looking for peace and prosperity, there is a smarter way to set goals. If we want to experience more joy in our lives, there is a smarter path we can follow. If relationships, balance, and purpose are important to us on our journey through life, then—

Somewhere along the way, we need to realize that we can use a S.M.A.R.T.E.R. system to achieve our goals and attain *SMARTER Success*.

 *Background and basis*

*T*o understand, discuss, and explain methods for becoming successful, one should have experienced the other end of the spectrum. I have. I was born broke. I came into the world penniless, just like you and every other naked baby. My parents were average and so was my childhood. I don't have a rags-to-riches story to share with you for inspiration. Yes, I am unique, just like everyone else. Sure, I have overcome adversity. So have you. The one thing I can offer you that no one else can is an explanation of success from my own personal perspective. It is a view of life and the world that I have developed while studying the ancient wisdom of a hundred sages and observing the simplicity of success in thousands of animals.

Animals are born with basic instincts. The only way they can increase their knowledge is to learn from experience. Through trial and error, making correct choices and mistakes, and discovering rewards and consequences, animals learn about the world in which they live and how they should interact with it.

People are born with few or no instincts. Like all animals, we learn by experience. But we also have the unique opportunity to learn from others. By reading words of wisdom, listening to voices of experience, and observing adventures of others, we can gain knowledge that will help us avoid negative consequences and enjoy the rewards of making smarter choices.

The collection of background information for this book began more than a quarter century ago when I applied for admission to veterinary college at Michigan State University. Friends warned that I should not get my hopes up for being admitted to vet school. My cousins said I would not or could not get into the professional program. Few of my relatives even went to college and we never had a doctor in our family. I was determined to try anyway.

In May of 1973, I received the good news. Michigan State University accepted me into their college of veterinary medicine. I beat the odds and accomplished a childhood dream. Out of the several hundred students who applied, I was among those accepted into the freshman class. And just as soon as I got into vet school, I started working to get out . . . with a diploma, of course.

During my junior year, I traveled to Europe and visited the Yorkshire, England, veterinary practice of James Wight, a.k.a. James Herriot. He was the author of *All Creatures Great and Small* as well as *All Things Bright and Beautiful* and several other books about English veterinarians and animals. Partially due to his influence, I decided that I did not want to spend my career working on just cows or just horses or just pets. I wanted the diversity of a rural general practice like Dr. Herriot's, a veterinary practice that would provide medical and surgical care for "Almost All Creatures Great and Small," which is the slogan I eventually coined for my clinic. The word "Almost" was added to allow for the exclusion of humans, insects, and obnoxious critters.

Veterinary school was difficult and I had to work diligently to earn good grades. The pressure to excel was relieved when one of the deans of the school, Dr. Hyram Kitchen, told me there was no correlation between grades and success. Many average students went into private practice and did exceptionally well. I didn't graduate *magna cum laude*, with high honors. I graduated *magna cum pellidentum*, largely by the skin of my teeth. But I had reached my goal. I had obtained a diploma as a doctor of veterinary medicine. I took an oath and became a gentle country doctor for pets and farm animals.

After graduation, I took the next step in the education process and started to apply what I had learned in school to everyday situations. My real-world adventures revealed all the knowledge that remained to be learned through experience. I continued to study and practice and learned a lot more about animals and a lot more about life. Working with animals from the time they were born till the time they died gave me a rich base of experience and knowledge. And I found that there was always something more to learn if I was willing to observe the world around me and absorb information.

> ### Veterinarian's Oath
> *Being admitted to the profession of veterinary medicine, I solemnly swear to use my scientific knowledge and skills for the benefit of society through the protection of animal health, the relief of animal suffering, the conservation of animal resources, the promotion of public health, and the advancement of medical knowledge. I will practice my profession conscientiously, with dignity, and in keeping with the principles of veterinary medical ethics. I accept as a lifelong obligation the continual improvement of my professional knowledge and competence.*

The early years in veterinary practice

While most of my classmates went to work for established veterinary clinics, I started my own private practice on the Monday after graduation. To build my practice in a rural community meant working twenty-four hours a day, seven days a week; animals never care about time clocks or calendars. In my first two years of practice I took only one weekend off for a two-day vacation. I have no regrets about how things began, but it probably was not the most intelligent way to live.

Over the past quarter century, I have had the opportunity to help all kinds of creatures. Assisting people with their pets and farm animals has been a privilege that I never take for granted. I have had the chance to prescribe medications and perform surgeries that saved thousands of lives and preserved the quality of life for countless others. In doing so, I have worked with more species of animals than I can remember. Most of the animals in my area were cows on dairy farms. Much of my time was spent helping the cows become pregnant and then delivering the baby calves when the birthing was difficult. I also worked with horses, pigs, sheep, goats, donkeys, mules, and several other types of farm animals. I helped dogs, cats, hamsters, rats, rabbits, and birds. A little local zoo called upon me to help their camels, zebras, cougars, lions, tigers, and bears. Whether it was helping an 1,800-pound Holstein cow, a gerbil that weighed ounces, or an animal of any size in between, whatever good I have done, I have never done it alone. I have always had support and assistance from other humans, higher powers, and of course, the patients themselves.

People become veterinarians to help animals, but we learn quickly that the profession requires us to work with other humans, too. People are needed for financial support of a veterinary practice. They are needed to aid with therapies. Owners of pets and livestock are responsible for the husbandry and care that are needed to keep animals sound and healthy.

Veterinarians also need patients who cooperate and respond appropriately to treatments. When animals give up the will to live, the prognosis is always hopeless. When animals refuse therapy, as with wild and zoo animals, diagnosis and treatment plans are extremely challenging. In some cases the vet is unable to do anything but observe the situation and try to prevent future events and episodes.

Veterinarians spend most of their careers studying animals, but because we ourselves are humans and we work with other humans, we learn a lot about people, too. The similarities between animals and people are remarkable, yet there are some major differences. One big difference is the way we think. Humans are the most intelligent creatures on earth and score higher than any other animal on intelligence tests. Of course, I.Q. tests are all created and administered by humans who are naturally biased. If animals designed the intelligence tests, humans might not fare as well.

Human beings have the most advanced central nervous systems. Our brains give us dominion over all the other animals on earth. Whether we are truly the smartest animals on earth depends not only on our ability to think, but also upon *how we think* and *what we think about*. Scientists speculate that we use only a small fraction of our brains, perhaps as little as 5 percent of our mental capacity—some people use much less. That leaves a lot of room for more thinking.

You only need to increase the amount of your brain that you use by a small percentage to increase your thinking ability a great deal. Your capacity to think new thoughts is unlimited. 🐾

I don't believe animals actually think about health, disease, and death very much. Most people do. Animals give up hope for recovery from an illness or injury only when their condition is terminal. People become hopeless even when their condition is temporary. People commit suicide with guns and knives and pills. People intentionally breathe or consume harmful chemicals like tobacco smoke, recreational drugs, and other poisons. Animals who actually want to die do so because of illness or injury that prevents further existence. People choose to die because of attitudes that develop from improper ways of thinking.

When it comes to health, humans may not be the smartest

For humans, where there is life there can be hope. Helplessness and hopelessness are mental states that can be changed by changing the way people think, which is simple, but not always easy. Humans may require counseling. Sometimes thought patterns in the brain go on so long that the actual chemistry of the brain changes. Sometimes prescription drugs are required to alter the chemistry of the brain and return it to a normal state of balance.

Drugs can help the brains of animals also, but no amount of talking can change how animals think. There is no amount of counseling that can change an animal's course once it has made up its mind to become hopeless and die. Fortunately, most creatures have very strong wills to live. Self-preservation is instinctive in most animals and they welcome help when they are ill.

The more I study animals and the people who care for them, the more I realize that thoughts influence health and disease. The human ability to think and process information can actually be beneficial to your health. It can also be deadly. I recommend books by authors like Steven Locke, Deepak Chopra, Bernie Siegel, Joan Borysenko, Maxwell Maltz, and Daniel Goleman if you want to learn more about the mind-body connection. They explore the topic thoroughly and can help you heal yourself, if you want to.

Good thinking can produce good health just as improper thinking can be hazardous to your health. Negative thoughts in your mind can produce negative consequences in your body. Thoughts are contributing factors in heart disease, high blood pressure, ulcers, and immune suppression. Thinking controls eating, and overeating can lead to obesity and all of the problems associated with excess weight. Many of the common human diseases and cancers are rare in the rest of the animal kingdom because animals seldom harbor negative thoughts. Human thinking interferes with the natural biological systems that influence the incidence of disease. Contemporary American habits and issues like smoking tobacco, overeating, self-intoxication, pill popping, poor self-esteem, hatred, and living with regret are rare in animals, as are the diseases they induce.

Life and death experiences

Delivering babies from all sorts of critters has always been the best part of my veterinary practice. I have untangled foals inside 2,000-pound draft horse mares and eased out baby bunnies from two-pound rabbits. I have used jacks and winches to pull calves out of cows and gentle, cautious traction to remove kittens from mother mountain lions. I have performed caesarean sections to surgically remove babies from seven-pound Chihuahuas and from 1700-pound milking cows. I even delivered my first son and a year later, his sister. It has been a great privilege to participate in the miracle of birth.

When animals got sick and were likely to die, I was able to prescribe medicine to help them back to a state of health. Sometimes just a small injection would make a big difference. Sometimes treatment meant getting a large pill into a small mouth that was lined with sharp teeth. Sometimes it meant wrestling with an animal that weighed twelve times what I did or stood twice my height.

Sometimes I needed to educate owners about animal care in order to help my patients stay healthy. There was little I could do for a patient who was not receiving proper food and shelter. Sometimes owners needed to learn about nutrition, ventilation, bedding, or water quality in order to keep their animals free of disease.

Occasionally a patient needed surgery so it could continue living. From the intestines of dogs I have removed steak bones that became lodged because they were not chewed completely. I have taken out tumors and growths and drained abscesses and hematomas. I have resected loops of bowel that had become twisted and blocked. I have removed stones over an inch in diameter from urinary bladders—stones that had formed from crystals of minerals in the urine. "A chance to cut was a chance to cure."

Trying to save lives was and is exciting, often very rewarding, and sometimes lots of fun. But a veterinarian's life is not always enjoyable. In addition to learning a lot about life, I also got a close look at death. Sometimes a patient failed to respond to a treatment. Rarely (once is too often), a pet failed to recover from surgery. Losing a patient was depressing. Every time an animal died, I felt that I had failed, even though I knew it was usually out of my control and not my fault.

Every practicing veterinarian sees patients who are terminally ill and others who have no chance to live a pain-free life. One of the saddest jobs in the profession is that of euthanasia, also called mercy killing. It is disheartening to dedicate one's life to saving lives and then be required to end them. As I have witnessed both life and death over the course of time, I have learned that there are fates worse than death. Euthanasia has changed my perspective of success and failure. I have come to realize that when done painlessly and with compassion and dignity, euthanasia can be regarded as a successful end to life.

The challenges of a rural veterinary practice were forever changing. One day I might see a lame guinea pig, a dog that was hit by a car, and 60 cows to check for pregnancy. The next day I might attend to a zebra that was shivering, a cat that couldn't pass water, a horse with a bellyache, and a dog who didn't want to eat. Tomorrow… more animals, more problems, and different challenges.

Because of my training in veterinary school, continuing education seminars after graduation, and reading hundreds of veterinary journals, I know a lot *about* animals. Because of my years of experience with almost all kinds of creatures, great and small, I also *know* animals—at least I know them better than I did years ago. There is big difference between knowing about animals and actually knowing animals. Likewise, we can know *about* life by studying biology and physiology and sociology, but we don't really *know* life until we experience it. Of course, no one can know it all, but we can share what we have learned and experienced.

Having lived a half century, I have experienced both happiness and hardships, like most other people. As a child I endured bouts with hepatitis, pneumonia, and two brothers. I have lived through abuse, obesity, and alcoholism. I have been divorced, broke, and depressed, and I'm pretty sure it happened in that order.

I once weighed 220 pounds. My girth became so large I had a hard time fitting into my coveralls. When examining and treating animals on farms, I wore lightweight jumpsuit coveralls over other clothes. The coveralls could be changed easily when they became soiled, which almost always happened. I once gained so much weight that my coveralls became very tight. I ripped out so many inseams while bending over that I tried to convince my wife that crotch-less coveralls were sexy.

In the days when I weighed over two hundred pounds, I could run a mile in less than thirty minutes. Actually, I jogged thirty yards at a time and then stopped to puff until I could waddle quickly again. I smoked tobacco in a pipe and occasionally drank alcohol in more than moderation. Yes, I also did other things I hope my children and parents never hear about. I wasn't very happy and I wasn't as healthy as I could have been.

At the top, but...

Somewhere along the way, I realized that I was at the top of my profession but not at peace with the world. With all of my success, I still had one problem: I wasn't really happy. I had accomplished my childhood dream of obtaining a college degree in veterinary medicine, but I was not satisfied. My practice had grown to provide me with great prosperity, but I was not content. I had acquired everything I ever dreamed of having and yet my life was not complete. I was still hungry. I wanted more. I wanted to climb higher. I thought I was pretty good at getting everything I ever wanted—yet I lacked something.

What do you do when you work very hard to get to the top in your field and then find that what you were looking for is not there? Perhaps I climbed the wrong ladder. Maybe I struggled up the wrong hill. Perhaps I wasn't sure what I was really after. I kept looking for that one thing that would satisfy my desire to be successful. Today, I realize what I lacked was not a thing at all but rather an attitude, a smarter way of thinking.

All through my childhood and young adulthood, becoming a veterinarian was my ultimate goal. I had never given much thought to what my goal would be once I earned my degree and established my own practice. As a veterinarian, I worked from day to day and started to wonder why I was doing what I was doing. My positive motivation for working toward a goal dissipated and was replaced by fear. I was motivated by the fear that my success might end. I was driven by the fear of failure. I became frustrated and depressed. It was a very dark period in my life. At one point I considered ending my life through suicide. That would have been easy as I had the all the drugs to do it properly and painlessly.

I began to see the light when I visited one of my mentors, Dr. Jeff Hamann. He grew up a decade before me in my hometown. He also went to Michigan State University and then returned home to practice with Dr. Paul Didion. I related to Dr. Hamann that I was being motivated solely by a fear of failure and saw no reason to continue doing what I was doing. When I asked him what motivated him to do the things he did in life, he didn't say a word but I could see he was pondering my question. After several minutes, he gave me an answer I shall always remember, but not for its intellectual acumen or rhetorical profundity. He simply said, "I don't know what drives me. I guess I just like doing what I'm doing." His answer seemed so simple that at first it disappointed me. Later, when I had time to consider it over the next few days, I realized I couldn't think of a better reason to do anything. His simple answer reminded me of why I wanted to be a veterinarian and especially why I wanted to go on doing what I was doing.

Sometimes life gets complicated and you can easily forget why you do what you do. Some people keep a journal or a diary so they can look back and remember. I use a poem. I recorded the challenges I encountered in veterinary medicine in a poem entitled, *To Be a Vet*. If you are interested in reading it, the poem is available at my website, Lippart.com.

Somewhere along the way I realized that if I wanted to improve my condition, I needed to change my thinking. I started by affirming personal responsibility for my past and present situations. I decided to take responsibility for my future and accept

You might write down some thoughts about your past and present adventures so that you will have something to read and remember if you ever forget why you are doing what you are doing.

the challenges I had received from numerous people. William H. Danforth, the founder of the Ralston Purina Company, dared me to be bigger than I was. Dale Carnegie told me to go out and win friends and influence people. Robert Schuller and Norman Vincent Peale inspired me to think positively and to live positively. And Wayne Dyer let me know that no one could pull my strings unless I let them. I learned from Louise Hay, Les Brown, Gerald Jampolski, and others to start changing my life by changing my way of thinking. I read and studied and listened. The more I learned the more I knew I had a lot more to learn. Denis Waitley related to me that all of the top achievers he knows are life-long learners. They are always looking for new skills, insights, and ideas. If they're not learning, they're not growing... not moving toward excellence.

I read and reread stories from the Bible and the Koran. I studied the writings of Buddha, Confucius, and Kahlil Gibran, especially his book, *The Prophet*. I read books on mind-body connections. I studied science, philosophy, metaphysics, ontology, epistemology, and theology. None of these sources alone gave me what I needed, but all influenced my way of thinking. When I put the ideas all together, I was content with my conclusions. I knew what I needed to do to make my life better.

I wanted to change. I wanted to take control of that change. I began the actions necessary to make the change. Physically, I ran for my life. By pushing myself to the limit of my endurance, I ran a mile without stopping. I jogged along the rural roads where I lived in the beautiful rolling countryside of Wisconsin. Sometimes I ran through the woods, sometimes through the pastures and the meadows. I set goals to run to the next hill and back. Then to the road sign in the distance. The next time I ran all the way to the lake and then back home. My knees hurt. My sore hip said, "Quit." When I felt pain, I rested, maybe for a few days. Then I ran again.

I put away my collections of smoking pipes and tobaccos. I shunned doughnuts and fatty foods. I drank water instead of soda. I ate smaller meals, and vitamin supplementation became a daily routine. Nutrition and thoughts of maintaining a healthy body gained priority.

My thoughts about health and happiness changed as I listened to inspirational lectures on audiotapes. I read a new self-help or self-improvement book every week. I continued to read many veterinary journals, but I also read contemporary and classic literature and absorbed as much of the wisdom as I could.

To change my life I studied the greatest thinkers and the most humble of animals. I wanted to learn what I could from them about creating a successful life. My research and exploration paid off big. The one most striking bit of knowledge I gleaned was the simplest fundamental law of the universe:

Thoughts are the basic building blocks of my world and nobody controls my thoughts, unless of course, I let them.

> *Without a thought, there is nothing. Thought is the intangible substance that makes up everything in our universe. Our world, and the world as perceived by every living creature, is nothing more than thoughts that are processed and stored within our minds and flow throughout our lives. This is a simple idea, but not easy to understand or apply to everyday life.*

Why should you read ideas about success written from a veterinarian's perspective? The answer is simple. One word. That's it: simple. After studying thousands of animals, reading hundreds of books on success and listening to as many speakers on the subject, I have found that the greatest secrets of success, the surest paths to prosperity, and the right roads to riches, are all simple. And many of the world's greatest ideas have natural animal origins.

What can we learn from animals about human life?

We are different. We are humans. Can there be anything the lower creatures can teach us? Is there something we can see in the way animals live and interact that can help us be successful? Can we improve our lives by observing animals? Can we become smarter by learning from ignorant animals? The answer to each question is simple. It is yes, *if we want to*.

> *By observing success in the animal world, we can discover a better way to look at success in the human world.* 🐾

If you are open to changing your ideas about goals and success, if you are willing to take responsibility for your future and make changes, *SMARTER Success* can enhance your life. If you believe that health and happiness are important, *SMARTER Success* will help you assure them both for a lifetime. If you want to make a positive impact on your own life as well as on the lives of the ones you love and cherish, *SMARTER Success* can help you along your path with health, happiness, peace, and prosperity.

 *Defining success*

Before you seek success, you should know what it is you are after. Before you begin any journey, you should know where you want to go. Ask yourself a few questions. What is success? Where do you find it? How do you get it? When will you find it? Is success something you really want? What will it cost?

What does success mean to you in each area of your life? How do you define success for your career, your health, your spiritual life, your family, your friends and your finances? Is each area equally important to you? Before you search for success in any area of your life, be sure you know what you are after and how it will affect the other areas.

The path to *SMARTER Success* begins with identifying what you want and why you want it. You can say that you want to be successful, but what does that really mean? The dictionary can give you a definition of success, your friends and family can let you know how they expect you to be successful, but your own personal definition is more important. Society, heritage, and culture can suggest what you need to do to become successful, but your own personal definition is what matters most. If you allow anyone else to set the

❖ "Success is peace of mind, which is a direct result of self-satisfaction in knowing you did your best to become the best that you are capable of becoming."
—John Wooden

standards by which you define success, then you will always be striving toward someone else's goals.

If you define success for yourself, you are an independent thinker. You are part of a select group of people who have taken the time to think about what they really want and what will really make them successful.

If you are still unsure about success but want to determine what success means to you as an individual, you are in another special group of people who are open to new ideas and thoughts about success and happiness. By studying and thinking about different ideas relating to success you will be better able to create or alter your own definition.

About 300 B.C., the great Greek philosopher Aristotle defined success as "self-contentedness." A Catholic monk I met defined success almost as simply—to him success meant consistently thinking happy thoughts. If each of your thoughts creates happiness, then you will have a happy life and be successful. Perhaps your definition is as simple and concise, or if that is not enough of a definition, you may want to expand it a little. Ralph Waldo Emerson elaborated on the subject when he wrote: "To earn the appreciation of honest critics and endure the betrayal of false friends; To appreciate beauty; To find the best in others; To leave the world a bit better, whether by a healthy child, a garden patch, or a redeemed social condition; To know even one life has breathed easier because you lived. This is to have succeeded."

My favorite definition of success comes from Earl Nightingale. He spoke and wrote volumes on the subject of success. He often said, "Success is the progressive realization of a worthy goal or ideal. It is not a destination. It is a journey—a daily event." To Earl Nightingale, success was not a position you reached in life; rather, it was the way you pursued your dreams.

I believe that two things in life are essential for success. They are very simple, yet often elusive. To me success means maintaining an optimal state of health and a most-of-the-time condition of happiness. No one can accumulate enough money, control enough power, attain high enough status, or collect enough toys to make life worthwhile if he or she isn't happy and healthy.

❧ "Success is to know what you are doing, to love what you are doing, and to believe in what you are doing."

—Will Rogers

Success seems simple to define, but it isn't always easy

The definition of success isn't always as obvious as it may seem. Thoughts about success in your family life might be different from success in your career. Your financial success might have a different meaning from your spiritual success or that of your relationships or health.

> *S uccess is relative—the more success, the more relatives.* ❀

Family success might mean lots of kids or a close extended family without any divorces or premature deaths. Perhaps you want two children, maybe twelve. Perhaps you want hundreds to attend your family reunions. Maybe you just want a significant other or one very close friend for your "family."

A successful career might mean working to climb a corporate ladder. Perhaps you are looking for a promotion or a raise. Success in business might mean running your own company. It might mean earning a service award or proficiency certificate. It might mean getting a gold watch for thirty years of service in one position or it might mean having thirty different jobs in as many years.

People want to be financially successful. An increase in wages or salary is usually welcomed. Most of us want to be RICH! We want our lottery tickets to provide us with millions of dollars. We want our sweepstake entries to identify us as the instant winners of enough money to let us retire in luxury. We want our stock portfolios and real estate investments to grow and increase our net worth. We want our inheritance to go through probate successfully when wealthy relatives pass away.

Religious success might mean someday going to heaven or to a utopian afterlife. To some success might mean a pilgrimage, visiting a holy shrine or place of religious history. It might mean progressing to a new level of being or consciousness. Some people define religious success as transcending mortal life.

❀ "Let us realize that the privilege to work is a gift, that power to work is a blessing, that love of work is success."

—David O. McKay

Successful relationships might mean having hundreds of close friends or it might mean being married to one person for fifty years. Perhaps you want to network and know thousands of people by name. Success might mean filling several boxes with business cards or having rows of Rolodex's on your desk. Or maybe it means simply having someone who is always there to give you a hand when you need help.

Successful health might mean living without drugs or it could mean living to be one hundred years old. It might mean simply living without pain. Health might mean staying out of hospitals and clinics. It might mean maintaining a body that is physically fit and a mind that is sharp and clear.

Defining success seems simple, but it isn't always easy. We often take shortcuts and allow others to define success for us. For example, success is often measured by one's vocation or profession. Doctors and lawyers and business owners are thought of as highly successful people. Yet many of them have marriages that fail and end in divorce. Depression and even suicide are health hazards within the professions. Professional people may look successful, but they too have areas in their lives that tend to get out of balance.

We look at celebrities and try to emulate their success, not realizing that they may be successful in a few aspects of their lives, but miserable failures in others. Fame, power, money, prestige, notoriety, respect, and admiration are the parameters by which we often measure success. Therefore, we think we want to have all that, too. We aren't sure how the rich and famous people got to where they are, but we dream of being there just like them. We want to be just as successful without knowing the price they had to pay for their success.

Perhaps the success you envision is not worth the price. Even those who have accomplished great things will occasionally admit that the achievements were not worth what they had to undergo and endure. If they had a chance to do the same things over again, many might not. An athlete might have a successful season by outperforming peers, but later end up without a job or means of support, sometimes with physical disabilities from sports injuries. A girl might go to Los Angeles and model clothes, jewelry, and makeup for which she would be paid large sums of money. She could be successful in the

---

❖ "The talent of success is nothing more than doing what you do well, and doing well whatever you do, without a thought of fame."

—Henry Wadsworth Longfellow

world of high fashion until she spent her money on drugs that changed her appearance enough that nobody even wanted to look at her.

Actors and actresses are successful in films and become movie stars. They also become famous for starting marriages that do not last very long. Professionally and financially they may be successful. But few become famous for maintaining relationships, health, or family success.

Politicians who win elections and lead states and nations are looked up to as being successful. One of the most successful politicians of the twentieth century rallied his followers to form armies that crushed cities and conquered countries. He was one of the most charismatic, motivational speakers in history. Few could compare with his success in government, leadership, and political power yet few would consider him a successful person in other areas of his life. Adolph Hitler left a legacy of being a despicable man who successfully built up and then destroyed millions of lives, including his own.

Sometimes great accomplishments can overshadow past failures and make people look successful. Could a man be thought successful if he abandoned his pregnant girlfriend? Imagine that after she gave birth to the child in a community miles away, he married her and together they had another child. They dreamed together and designed tremendous plans for making major advances and contributions to the world. As they worked together toward a mutual goal, she just as hard as he, the man then left his wife for another woman. He eventually received the credit and fame for being one of the most intelligent people on earth while the abandoned wife raised the children. Years ago, some might have called Albert Einstein a deserter of his family. Today, we regard him as a successful scientist—a genius. He was certainly successful in one aspect of life, his career, but perhaps not so successful with his family or relationships.

Many people throughout history have appeared to be very successful, but they did not consider themselves to be so. Meriwether Lewis of the Lewis and Clark expedition was one of history's greatest American explorers. He suffered through hunger and bitter cold to search uncharted land for a route between Missouri and the Pacific Ocean. When he reached his destination and returned in the early 1800s, President Thomas Jefferson rewarded him with money, property, and official titles. By most standards, he was a great success.

😺 "There is only one success—to be able to spend your life in your own way."
—Christopher Morley

His name will be in history books for all time as a tremendously successful explorer, yet the man never seemed to feel successful. His life ended with a probable suicide involving alcohol just a few years after his great discoveries.

> *What other people think of you is important. But ultimately, success depends upon what you think of yourself. If you don't think you are successful, it will matter little what others think of you.*

Edwin Armstrong discovered FM radio waves in the 1930s at a time when other scientists rejected their importance. In addition to FM (frequency modulation), Armstrong discovered and patented inventions in hi-fi broadcasting and made improvements to long-range radar and communications. He was an extremely successful scientist. Everybody in the radio business, including RCA, Zenith, Philco, Magnavox, Motorola, and Crosley, made fantastic profits using Armstrong's inventions while he received very little compensation. Instead of accepting one million dollars for his ideas, he litigated for more. After years and years of court battles, Armstrong lost his fight against the wealthy companies. Exhausted and enraged, he fell into hopelessness and despair. On February 1, 1954, he put on his hat and coat and walked out the window of his thirteenth floor apartment. Ultimately for Armstrong, money and fame were more important than life itself.

> *No matter how great the people of the world believe you are, you can never be more successful than you think yourself to be.*

The people throughout history who appeared to be successful yet took their own lives are countless. Surely you recognize many of the names on the following list:

John Belushi
George Eastman
Freddie Prinze
Vincent van Gogh

☙ "Success is not in the destination. It is in earning the right to be there."
—Eric Butterworth

Elvis Presley
Marilyn Monroe
Kurt Cobain
Sid Vicious
Janis Joplin
Jim Morrison
Jimi Hendrix
Paul Williams
Vinnie Taylor
Pete Ham
John Panozzo
Steve Clark
Bon Scott

These are people whom you would consider to have been successful. Yet their lives ended because of their lack of happiness in simply living.

Many people reach the pinnacle of their profession—the top of their talent, the summit of financial freedom, the peak of parenthood, the crest of creativity—and they are still not content. They don't feel successful because they never really defined success for themselves. Or they defined success as the accumulation of material things and were still not satisfied when they obtained the things they thought would make them happy.

If success is eluding you, it is possible you need to alter your view of success. If you are not as happy as you could be because you don't feel successful, perhaps you need to change your definition of success. This doesn't mean that you should lower the bar or your standards for success. Rather, it means you might consider looking at a totally different bar. You might be reaching for something that really won't fulfill your life. A different bar or a different goal might not only be easier, it might also be more natural for you.

Definitions change as you age

When I was a teenager, my father told me a tall tale about the time his dad found a talking frog by the river near their home. My elderly grandfather was

❧ "The road is always better than the inn."

—Cervantes

astonished when the frog said, "Kiss me and I will turn into a beautiful young lady. I will be eternally grateful to you and do anything you want." Grandpa put the frog in a box and took it into the house.

I asked my father if Grandpa kissed the frog. If I could have changed a frog into a pretty girl who would be indebted to me, I would kiss her very quickly. To me that would be a dream come true. As it turned out, Grandpa didn't share my perspective. The frog itself fulfilled Grandpa's fantasies. At his elderly age he didn't want a beautiful babe; he preferred to have a talking frog for conversation.

Just as my grandfather and I had different views of the frog, we all look at success differently at different ages in our lives. There seems to be a cycle as to how we define success. When we are very young, success means keeping our underwear dry. When we are a few years older, success means crossing a busy street without help. When we are adolescents, success means getting a date for Saturday night. A few years later it means graduation and a wedding. Next, success means having a career and a family. The family grows up and we find success to mean more graduations and more weddings. Moving into the golden years, success means getting a date for Saturday night (with a spouse if you have one) and making it across a busy street without help. When we reach our final years, success might mean keeping our underwear dry. The cycle of the definition of success is then complete.

People have viewed success differently in different eras in time. Centuries ago, success simply meant having enough to eat and not being eaten. Anyone who lived past thirty years of age was quite successful, by our ancestors' definition. Today, food, clothing, shelter, and a television are staples of average families. Simply staying alive and being free from hunger are seldom considered parameters of success.

Admittedly, starvation and homelessness are still a part of our culture. In America, however, those who are overweight and obese grossly outnumber the people who are starving. The homeless are few compared with the number of people who live in adequate housing. It is a sad commentary on our society that we may have more shelters for stray dogs in our communities than we do for stray people.

❖ "Success means accomplishments as the result of our own efforts and abilities. Proper preparation is the key to success. Our acts can be no wiser than our understanding."
—George S. Clason

Two generations ago, my maternal grandfather's family came to America from Germany as common laborers. Eventually, they bought a farm and Grandpa became a dairyman. Farming was a simple way of life, but it wasn't easy. He stooped next to the cows and milked them by hand. He spread manure with a wagon and a team of horses in the heat of the sun and the frosty chill of blowing snow. He got together with the neighbors to thresh grain in the fall and share food in the winter. He didn't have a phone, electricity, or indoor plumbing in the early years of his farming career. Nevertheless, he was as successful as any farmer in his area of the county.

Times have changed. Today, people stand upright in parlors to milk cows and push buttons to move feed and manure. Farming is a bit easier, but not nearly as simple. The definition of successful farming appears to have changed with the times. In Grandpa's day, his farm was thought to be successful. If he were still farming today with his twelve cows and eighty acres of cropland, he would be considered old-fashioned and obsolete compared with modern dairies that have hundreds of cows.

Even the definition of a successful veterinary practice can change

Years ago I defined a successful veterinary practice differently from the way I do today. When I was fresh out of college, I dreamed of creating an ideal veterinary practice, including:

- Five doctors who would work for me. Each would create income and I would receive a percentage of their profit.
- Twelve veterinary technicians who would assist the doctors and increase their efficiency and productivity.
- An office that would be well staffed with several receptionists, a business manager, and other employees.
- A toll-free telephone number that would encourage people from all over the country to call my clinic for diagnoses, therapies, and advice.
- Thousands of clients who would bring their animals to my clinic.

🐾 "Success is diligent effort toward a focused goal."

—Ed Germond

My goal once was to build such a practice. I renovated an old dairy barn on a little farm just outside of a town with a population of 1,350. There were thousands of cows on the farms in the area, which made it a good location for a practice servicing the needs of "Almost All Creatures Great and Small." The building had two floors with four thousand square feet of space on each floor. It was huge for my needs, but the dairy industry was growing quickly and I envisioned my practice doing the same.

Within a short period of time, I hired an associate. Two years later, three doctors were needed to complete all the work and meet the demands of the clients. I hired more secretaries, receptionists, veterinary technicians, and kennel help. Revenue increased faster than I expected. So did the problems.

Some clients complained about the new vets in the practice and didn't want them working with their animals ever again. A couple of clients preferred the new vets and didn't want *me* working with their animals again. The phone rang at all hours of the day and night, especially when my family was planning to do something special. The doctors argued about therapies and fees and salaries. Intra-office friction led to disgruntled employees. Staff members quit and had to be replaced. Time spent running the business exceeded time spent helping the animals.

I guess all that meant I was successful.

My clientele increased in number to the point where I knew only half of the people for whom I worked. I didn't have time to get to know my clients or my patients. Some customers had charge accounts at the clinic and never paid them off before filing bankruptcy. And there seemed to be less time for personal relationships with my family and friends.

The practice grew to the point where it was controlling my life. Instead of running my practice, my practice was running me. I wanted to get out of operating a business and get back to helping animals and the people who loved them. I needed to regain control of my situation and reevaluate my definition of a successful practice. I realized that what I had earlier believed was the ideal veterinary practice was no longer valid. What I thought was success was no longer success, at least for me.

❧ "I know the price of success: dedication, hard work and an unremitting devotion to the things you want to see happen."

—Frank Lloyd Wright

> *Perhaps success is something you don't spend much time thinking about because you think you know all there is to know about success. As with anything, there is always more that you can learn.*

Numbers make success easy to define

Success is easy to define when there are clearly visible goals, as in sports. Success is simple to determine when you keep score by numbers. Success is objective in games like football, baseball, soccer, and hockey. Winning teams rack up higher numbers than their opponents do. They are the most successful.

Some sports like golf also keep score with numbers, but winners have the fewest strokes. The most successful players have the lowest scores.

Success is easy to determine in games played with cards. Numbers and suits keep score and measure success in games of poker, bridge, cribbage, euchre, and countless other card games. Players keep score and determine success with numbers, points, or pegs.

Numbers and positions determine the winner in board games with chutes and ladders, trivia questions, or real estate transactions. The one who wins by the rules of the game is the most successful.

Success in a race is very easy to measure. Runners, swimmers, horses, dogs, and cars are numbered as they finish the race. Winners cross the finish line ahead of the rest. The first one to finish the race is the most successful.

Results of political elections are easily determined by counting the number of votes cast (unless you live in a state where problems are encountered with voter registration, ballots, counters, and chads). The candidate with the greatest number of votes wins and is successful.

Objective results make it easy to measure success, but in some sports like gymnastics, figure skating, diving, and dressage, success is more subjective. Judges decide which contestant performs or competes the best. Their opinions determine success. The results are open to criticism and controversy but a score still determines who wins. When numbers are used to measure success, the winner is clearly identifiable.

❖ "Success seems to be connected with action. Successful people keep moving. They make mistakes, but they don't quit."

—Conrad Hilton

In our day-to-day lives, personal success is measured with numbers as in sports and politics. That is natural because we are accustomed to measuring with numbers. Instead of keeping track of points or votes, money is used to measure success. Superficially, money and the things money can buy are the benchmarks of success. Success is often defined or described by how many things we can accumulate with our money.

Half a century ago (when it was still politically acceptable to say such things) a male made this comment about success. He said, "A man is successful when he makes more money than his wife can spend." That statement might get a laugh, but it seems sexist today because it assumes that the man is the income earner in the family. Before you condemn the guy who said that, realize that his statement was followed up by a female saying, "A woman is successful when she can find such a man."

Author and professional speaker Zig Zigler, once told me, "Money is not the most important thing in life, but it is right up there with oxygen." There is little doubt that money makes the world go around. Money is easy to count. Money is easy to exchange for services or products or old debts. Money can make things happen.

> *When money is the measure of success, even thieves are successful if they can steal enough money.* 🐾

As a society, we buy into the idea that to be successful we have to collect a lot of stuff. The more stuff we collect, the more successful we are. He who dies with the most toys wins. To be successful in America, we have to have money because that is how we measure success. The more money you have, the more successful you are. The most popular measurement of success is cash in the bank. Net worth determines status, esteem, power, position, and prestige. Right?

If you make more money than I do, you are more successful.

If you live in a bigger house, you are more successful.

🐾 "There are no secrets to success. Don't waste time looking for them. Success is the result of perfection, hard work, learning from failure, loyalty to those for whom you work, and persistence."

—Colin Powell

If you drive a bigger, faster, newer, or more expensive car, you are more successful.

If you have jewelry that is brighter, larger, or more sparkly, you are more successful.

If you own a motor home, a vacation cottage, a boat, or an airplane, you are more successful.

Right?

These generalizations are all quite close to being correct, but that doesn't make them right.

Does money measure success in your life?

If money measures success and if success means happiness, then the wealthiest people should be the happiest people. But are people with two million dollars twice as happy as those with only one million dollars?

We are living in the wealthiest nation on earth. We are the richest humans in history. Americans have about the highest standard of living in the world. There is a greater difference between the standard of living for a third world citizen and an average American than there is between the average and wealthiest Americans. By most standards of the world, we are all successful. It follows that we should already be the happiest people on the planet. But are we?

If we are so rich, why aren't we all happy? We consume more antidepressants than any other population. We get depressed and some of us commit suicide. That's not natural. Happy people don't want to kill themselves.

> *Rich people who are unhappy are not as well off as poor people who are unhappy. The poor people can at least wish for the money they think will change their condition.*

We are making a living, but are we neglecting to make a life that is worth living? Do possessions make us successful? Does having stuff create happiness? Does owning property, building a large bank account, or accumulating a stock portfolio determine health or just wealth? Does money make

❖ "Success is having a flair for the thing that you are doing; knowing that is not enough, you have got to have hard work and a sense of purpose."
—Margaret Thatcher

us feel good over the length of our lives? Can wealth alone secure peace of mind?

Why do so many marriages end in divorce? We have multiplied our possessions, but we have divided our families. We live in fancy houses but come from broken homes. We have learned how to split an atom but we can't keep our marriages together. Mothers are earning incomes like fathers, but many parents don't live together any more.

We have been able to start a pregnancy in a laboratory Petri dish, but we can't prevent pregnancies in our teenage daughters. We have mapped the sequences of amino acids in our DNA's (deoxyribonucleic acids), but we are unable to halt the spread of STD's (sexually-transmitted diseases).

Why are so many people searching for more when they have so much already? We've got it all; yet we seem to be lacking. We have more conveniences; yet we end up with less time. We seem to be working very hard for things we don't have time to use. We own more boats, cycles, skis, snowmobiles, four-wheelers, electronic toys, cottages, campers, and recreational vehicles, but we enjoy them less.

We have computers and cell phones that can communicate across the country or around the world in just seconds. However, we can't find the time to talk with the members of our families, as we know we should. We neglect to call our friends as we said we would. We don't communicate with each other as well as we could.

> *If we are what we eat, then many of us have become easy, fast, and cheap.* 🐾

We can choose from more kinds of food in the aisles of every store, but many of our choices contain less natural nutrition than ever before. We prepare more food than we can possibly consume, and we eat until we become obese. We quickly eat fast food that slowly eats away at our health by diminishing our natural nutritional reserves.

We love to spend money. We owe more and continue to abuse credit. If we don't have enough money to buy the things that make us appear successful, we

🐾 "Success is going from failure to failure without losing enthusiasm."
—Winston Churchill

purchase merchandise with a plastic card or borrow against our future pay-checks.

> *Daytime television dramas may not portray real life but they support the idea that wealth does not create happiness. Most television stories are based upon the trials and tribulations of wealthy and physically beautiful people who may appear successful but are not very happy. The plots are full of conflict, sadness, and unhealthy rich people. Ironically, the commercials between the stories continue to propagate the myth that you can buy success if you have enough money.*

We are exploring outer space, but are losing touch with our inner space. We have been all the way to the moon and back, but we have trouble crossing the road to meet our new neighbors.

Why is there such a high turnover of employees in businesses? People jump like kangaroos from job to job searching for more benefits, higher salaries, and easier employment. Steep profits are being taken, but shallow relationships are being formed.

Our cities have taller buildings, while our citizens possess shorter tempers. Our interstate road system provides us with wider highways, but the drivers have narrower minds. We have broader networks of acquaintances, but our friendships seem to be as disposable as do many of our other modern conveniences. We have mostly abolished segregation, but prejudice remains.

We watch too much television, drink too much, smoke too much, spend too recklessly, drive too fast, get angry too quickly, stay up too late, and get up too tired. We laugh too little, pray too rarely, read too infrequently, love too seldom, and hate too often. We live extended lives, but don't get along with our extended families. We offer our children more knowledge, but less judgment and common sense. We have more experts, but more problems that require expertise for solutions. We have more medicines, but less wellness.

We go on measuring success with money while few notice that money measures only our material wealth. Outside of finances, success is seldom something that can be measured. Money cannot measure the success of our families, friendships, or spiritual lives.

❖ Rob Gilbert offers four surefire rules for success: show up, pay attention, ask questions, don't quit.

Perhaps it is time for us to change our perception of success, realign our priorities, restore proper balance in our lives, and regain a proper perspective. Maybe we have been chasing the wrong goals. Maybe we need to pursue goals to *be* more rather than to *have* more. As Henry Miller said, "If there is to be any peace it will come through being, not having." Perhaps it is time to reevaluate the definition of success.

> *Definitions of success change but the laws of success stay the same. In his uplifting little book, A Better Way to Live, Og Mandino writes, "Like the laws of nature, gravity, and physics, the true principles of success have been with us for thousands of years. They have never changed!" The laws of success are unchanged, but our interpretation of those laws, as well as the very definition of success, will change as we alter our perceptions.*

Changing ideas about success

Every once in a while I am struck with a new idea that seems to make real sense. I can't say I ever had a real epiphany or a mystic revelation. Somewhere along the way, I simply stumbled upon simple ideas that seem to explain life in a logical way.

One such idea came about while I was driving in my mobile veterinary clinic, a recreational vehicle I used as a veterinary clinic to offer better service to clients in a town fifteen miles away from my hospital. I was chatting with my part-time assistant, Kathy, as we were traveling. Kathy was always bubbly and energetic. Just a week earlier, her mother had come up to me in a local restaurant to tell me how much Kathy liked working a few hours a week in my clinic.

Kathy willingly told anyone why she was so happy. She and her husband owned a modest home near her parents who lived on a lake. Her kids were relatively healthy. Her family had a smart dog and a dependable car, and her husband had a good job.

Kathy's family life was not really typical for our area. Kathy quit her job in the local dental office when her first child was born. Since then she had been a stay-at-home mom, a volunteer at the church and at the school, and a

🐾 "Success is to be measured not so much by the position that one has reached in life as by the obstacles that one has overcome while trying to succeed."
—Booker T. Washington

member of several civic organizations. Kathy lived the life of a middle-class American female in the 1950s. In the 1990s, most women in our area had jobs outside their homes to help make ends meet. I wondered how she could afford to stay home. Didn't the family need a second full-time income?

It was springtime and Kathy was telling me of the vacation she and her husband had planned for the family. As she started talking about it, I had all I could do to hold back a burning question. I knew her husband worked at a farm implement dealership. I didn't think people in his industry were paid exceptionally well. I knew she was very conservative when purchasing food, clothing, and entertainment for the family, but how could they get by on just one salary? How could they afford a vacation? How come she had the apparent luxury of staying at home? She got to play and work with her children every day rather than go to a job she hated like so many other spouses. I wanted to ask her just how much money her husband made.

I didn't ask the bold money question. Their family income was really none of my business. But I still wanted to understand how they could get by on the income of one parent and the little I paid her as a part-time employee. What was their secret method of balancing their dreams and finances?

It all began to make sense when I remembered talking with another stay-at-home mom the previous week. Jill was very involved with school activities and kids, her own boy and girl and their friends. She told me that she would have to go back to work soon. The kids were getting older—twelve and fourteen—and the family was having a hard time making ends meet with just her husband's salary. She went on to say that if the family was going to maintain its lifestyle, they needed a second income. At first I was sympathetic, as I could relate to her situation. I have been there, and I am sure that many other people have, too.

Then I remembered that Jill and her family lived on a large lake. They had a ski boat, a sailboat, a jet ski, and other toys, and taxes that were substantial for the luxury house they owned. I didn't have any desire to ask Jill what their income was. Her husband was an attorney. I knew what his fees were, and I had a good idea of how much money he made.

❖ "That best portion of a good man's life: his little, nameless, unremembered acts of kindness and love."

—William Wordsworth

Kathy and Jill were two stay-at-home moms who lived in the same community. They had very different incomes and appeared to have very different ideas about money and how much they needed to be happy. One was content with little compared with the other who had much more and yet felt needy. My conversations with these women motivated me to take a closer look at my own definitions of success. I wondered how much is enough? How big must my house be? How many cars, boats, and toys do I need to collect? What standard of living do I require to be happy? Would I be happier if I had more money or if I spent more time with my family? When I answered these questions, I knew I had found the right path to success.

> *Money does not create success, but successful people always seem to have enough money.*

A new successful veterinary practice

I am amazed at how much my perception of a successful veterinary practice has changed over the quarter of a century I have been in practice. I used to think bigger was better. Many veterinary clinics have elaborate facilities, thousands of clients and patients, and ten to thirty people working together on the staff in harmony and cooperation. I have colleagues in those practices who appear to be very happy. Larger practices might be more successful for some veterinarians, but for me, bigger is not better.

I used to think a successful practice meant having a toll-free telephone number. I now have one, but sometimes wish I had an unlisted number, especially at home. Then, only my best clients would have access to me after regular business hours.

I used to think I needed thousands of clients. I now have a moderate number of clients for whom I deeply enjoy working. They respect my time, pay me well, and appreciate my services.

I used to think success was having a large group of associate veterinarians. I now like practicing by myself. No one is looking over my shoulder (except for students who work with me occasionally and keep me on my toes with all

---

🐾 "The valuables we possess are worthless if we forsake our personal values to obtain them. Without integrity we have nothing."

—Vetdini

sorts of interesting questions). There are no associates with whom I need to argue or split profits or share losses. There are no clients who come into my clinic and prefer "the other doctor." I charge a fee that I believe is fair and feel no pressure to meet a production quota.

I used to think a larger staff was better. I now realize that more employees can mean more conflict. With only one full-time employee and several part-timers, I have fewer personalities with whom I interact. Communication among employees is clear and concise.

For over a decade, I have been working to create my current definition of a successful practice. I like how my definition is changing. I will never have a perfect practice, but I enjoy working in a practice that is, at least by my definition, very successful.

> *Success needs to be defined, described, and imagined by the person who seeks it if it is to be personally worthwhile. Only the person pursuing success can describe it properly.*

Perhaps you are like I was when I was younger and you don't spend much time thinking about the meaning of success. It is easy to allow others to tell you what success *should* mean—success is just a condition in which you collect more stuff than you had yesterday. Success comes from comparing yourself with others. Success is having more possessions than your neighbors, friends, or rivals. When you stop to really think about success, these definitions are insufficient. They relate only to artificial parameters of success. They exclude the natural measures of success, which are not always obvious but are always more rewarding in the end.

What is success?

Sometimes a word transcends even the best definition we might find in a dictionary. The concept of success is different for each individual. What the dictionary dictates or what people say can offer you ideas, but ultimately you have to define success for yourself.

❧ Brian Tracy suggested we need the following for success: Freedom from fear, guilt, and anger; peace of mind; health and energy; loving relationships; financial freedom; personal fulfillment; self-actualization.

To help you understand the complexity of success, take a look at another word that is just as challenging to define. You have probably thought much more about trying to define the word "love" than the word "success." Both words are used freely, often without much thought of what they really mean. Just as everyone wants to feel successful, everyone wants to enjoy the feeling of love. In some ways, success is just as hard to describe as love. Unfortunately, we seldom take the time to think about what either really means.

Poets and songwriters have tried to describe love since the beginning of time. The dictionary offers over a dozen definitions. You and I would define love differently if we tried. We each have our own ideas of love based upon our experiences and perceptions.

If you ask a young person, "What is the opposite of love?" the child is likely to respond by saying, "The opposite of love is hate." That seems like a logical answer. Direct the same question to a person who has been married for some time and that person is likely to say, "The opposite of love is indifference."

Likewise, you could describe success as being the opposite of failure. But what then is failure? It is as hard to define failure as it is to define success. Countless events originally called failures later illuminated the paths to unbelievable inventions, discoveries, and victories. Before Thomas Edison created a practical light bulb, he

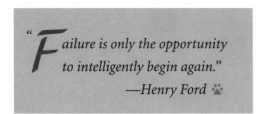

"*Failure is only the opportunity to intelligently begin again.*"
—Henry Ford

burned up thousands of filaments successfully identifying ideas that would not work. Robert Fulton had many disasters before he changed Fulton's Folly into a working steamboat. Many other inventors (perhaps most) experimented with possibilities that did not work before they hit upon an invention worthy of a patent.

I don't particularly like the word failure. Failure is a seven-letter "f" word that should be stricken from use like the infamous four-letter "f" word. To label anything a failure is to pass judgment and it is not always clear if results are good or bad. The word failure should be reserved for two classes of people: those who thought and never did, and those who did and never thought.

I do like what Oprah Winfrey has been quoted as saying about failure: "I will tell you that there have been no failures in my life. I don't want to sound like some metaphysical queen, but there have been no failures. There have been some tremendous lessons."

> "*If you have made mistakes, even serious ones, there is always another chance for you. What we call failure is not the falling down but the staying down.*"
> —*Mary Pickford* 🐾

Let's eliminate the use of the word failure and think of any outcome as just a result. For most experiences, the word failure should be replaced with "successful identification of a solution that did not work." If you try and don't succeed, you have successfully identified a way that did not work. Failing is not the opposite of succeeding—quitting is. The only way you can be deemed a real failure is to quit. The price you pay for success is insignificant compared with the price you pay for quitting.

Failure need not be a permanent condition. It can be only a temporary setback, if you keep trying. Failure should be your teacher, not your undertaker. As one poet said, "Failure is delay, not defeat. It is a temporary detour, not a dead-end street."

If your goal is to fail, and you succeed, are you a failure or a success?

If you want to live an extra-ordinary life, you have to live extra-ordinary days by thinking extraordinary thoughts. To be successful, you won't need to be better than anyone else or even to be like anyone else. By endeavoring to improve your present self, you will create a future that is beyond your current expectations. Tomorrow can be better than anything you can imagine today. Your destiny may well be beyond your present comprehension.

The past can't be changed. This may be true, but how you perceive it is entirely up to you. How you judge the past and what you pursue in the future depends on your perspective. The way you look at success and failure is up to you. I can't define success for you. I can't tell you what to think, but I do suggest that you think. Think about what success means to you.

The best things in life are free. The best thoughts are priceless.

A special way of looking at success

*O*ne of the most significant goals in my life is very simple. I want to encourage my children to develop their potential. My kids don't have to grow up to be what I expect them to be. However, I do expect them to mature and to live worthwhile lives. My job as a parent is to help them develop in a direction that will benefit themselves and the world in which they live. I want my children to be good people—honorable, happy, and healthy. I have always encouraged them to be successful. However, they are encouraged to define success for themselves and excel as they may.

Humans never completely become what they are capable of becoming. But where there is life there is hope. Hope allows us to believe that improvement is possible. If better is possible, best loses meaning. As long as people apply themselves, invest their talents in some worthwhile purpose, and make improvements in their lives, they are developing in a positive direction. My kids don't have to go to college or make piles of money in business to be successful. I just want them to be better tomorrow than they were today.

My father, a schoolteacher, told me when I was young that I could grow up to be anything I wanted to be…except a schoolteacher. Although it is a profession I have always held in high regard, Dad thought there had to be a better way to make a living and he didn't want his children to follow in his shoes. As for my children, they don't have to follow in my footsteps to please me, either. Actually, I realized when my kids were quite young that none of my three children would ever become a veterinarian. They accompanied me on farm visits and hung around the veterinary clinic daily. I think seeing so many sick animals and surgeries when they were toddlers overwhelmed them. The youngsters experienced more veterinary medicine in the first half-decade of life than most people will ever witness in a half-century. Their interest in medicine burned out before it started to kindle.

I believe I'm like most parents in that I want my children to be successful. I want them to be winners. And I want to protect them from failure. The way we define success and failure as parents or children will vary depending upon our points of view, but we all want our children to be successful at whatever they do. A story about my middle child, Michelle, offers one more perspective of success for your consideration.

Michelle was popular, self-confident, and poised, characteristics that got her elected class president all four years in high school. She was a joiner and a leader, and she liked to participate. But she was not particularly athletic, so when she went out for sports, I became concerned. Personally, I didn't believe that there was any way she could be a star or even come close to winning in athletic competitions. I didn't want to see her get hurt physically or psychologically. Therefore, I didn't encourage her to become involved with sports, but I didn't stand in her way, either.

Michelle's activities and involvement in sports helped me understand success from her adolescent perspective. Michelle wanted to go out for the cross-country team when she was in seventh grade. Although she was physically fit and had an athletic build, her body was designed with short legs. (When Michelle was a senior in high school, a fifth-grader asked her how old she was. When Michelle said she was eighteen, the youngster replied, "Wow! Is that all the bigger you're gonna get?")

Please don't misunderstand me. Michelle had a very attractive, proportionate figure. She was not short-legged like a basset or a dachshund, but she was no greyhound either! She was more like a miniature collie. Shelties (the proper name for small dogs that look like collies) are beautiful in their own way. But she was running against full-grown Lassies! How could she ever dream of winning?

At this point in a classic success story, the scenario would detail how Michelle overcame her short-legged challenges. Her struggle to pass her classmates on the racecourse would be described. The thrill of her victory over girls from other schools would inspire readers to overcome their deficiencies. The memorable motivational story would conclude with Michelle winning the state championship or something. Well, this story doesn't go that way at all. This story is not about winning in the end. Michelle's story is about winning all along the way.

Michelle was blessed with a body that could run—and run she did. She trained as hard as any of her teammates. Every day after school, the girls jumped into the school van. The coach drove them a few miles outside the city limits to a safe country road, opened the doors, and told them to run back to town. They had to run fast if they wanted to get back to the school before dinnertime.

To many people, Michelle was not considered a running success. She was not the star of the team. She didn't break any records. She was delighted to win a couple of medals for placing fifth or ninth. Sometimes, there were as many as 160 girls in a race! Most of the runners, the overwhelming majority of them, never won a race. The points each runner tallied seldom earned her team a victory. Yet, they weren't a team of losers. Simply having the chance to participate in the competition seemed to be more important than winning for Michelle and her teammates.

Cross-country is a sport that is different from most others. Each member of the team plays the same position. There are no quarterbacks or wide receivers. There are no forwards or centers or guards. There are no pitchers, no catchers, no fielders. There are no goal posts, hoops, or nets. Cross-country has a starting line, course markers, and one goal—the finish line. The cross-country team acts like a traditional healthy family: each member supports and encourages the others. They can easily relate to one another because they have so much in common. They are running. They are all in the same races, running by themselves to improve their personal bests, yet competing as a team. They even support opponents by encouraging them when passing in a race.

Coming in less than first is not failure in cross-country running. Everyone knows that only one runner will cross the finish line first, unless, of course, the runners are close enough to hold hands. Each girl is given her individual time at the end of a race, and success is realized whenever someone beats her own previous best time. The winner of the race crosses the finish line first, but the high school runners have different ways of measuring success. They have competitions within competitions. Who finished first from our school? Who improved her score the most? Did a freshman beat a senior? Who ran fast enough to make the varsity squad for the next race? How did the team do as a whole?

Michelle helped me to understand success. Sometimes, maybe most times, it was more important to participate than to win. She and her teammates developed their skills and courage in a spirit of sharing and joy. That made them all winners.

Competition in running races motivates improvement. Running is probably the oldest of competitive athletic events. In 776 B.C., the Olympic games started in Greece with running races. Even today, the Olympic games begin with a runner carrying a torch into the arena. The Olympic games are a special competition for wonderful athletes.

In 1968 A.D., a variation of the old Greek games was created as a wonderful competition for special athletes. The games are called Special Olympics and they exemplify the spirit of sports. In these games, success is not determined by who finishes first. Being first is not as important as participating and doing one's best. Eunice Kennedy Shriver, the sister of President John F. Kennedy, Bobby Kennedy, and Ted Kennedy, founded this special competition for children and adults with mental retardation. These games offer special people opportunities to develop physical fitness, demonstrate courage, experience joy, and participate in a sharing of gifts, skills, and friendship with their families, other Special Olympics athletes, and their communities. In most cases, Special Olympics is the only chance for these individuals to experience the joy of sports.

About twenty five thousand communities in the United States have Special Olympics programs. Nearly 150 countries have accredited Special Olympics programs, with more being developed around the world. Millions of children and adults have participated in Special Olympics.

Participating in Olympic games, running cross-country in high school, or just seeing who can run across a field the fastest can challenge us to improve. It can also help us understand success. A simple race can help us determine the meaning of success. Winning can be wonderful, but success doesn't have to mean coming in first.

If we could all play the game of life with that attitude, we could compete without conflict. We could all be winners with no one whining in defeat. We could strive

> *The motto of Special Olympics is, "Let me win. But if I cannot win, let me be brave in the attempt."* 🐾

for success and never suffer failure. If we could enjoy life as much as participants and volunteers enjoy Special Olympics, we would more fully appreciate the opportunities we have just to participate in life. We would value our chance simply to *be*. Perhaps we would not argue who is best. We would instead discuss who is getting better. Instead of fighting to win a battle, we would simply defend the right to play in the game.

Of course participation means taking risks, but that is necessary for success. The great tennis player Arthur Ashe once said, "You have got to get to the stage in life where going for it is more important than winning or losing." If we participate, at least we have the chance to improve and be successful in making an attempt. If we choose just to sit on the sidelines, we may never know or develop our real capabilities.

Athletes like Michelle and those who participate in Special Olympics can offer us a unique and healthy perspective of success. We can't all be number one in every contest, but we can all be brave in the process. We can all be winners in our own lives if we choose to strive for improvement and set SMARTER goals to be better people—not better than someone else, but better than our former selves.

Blissology—the study of lifelong happiness

Your personal definition of happiness is essential in your quest for success. If you agree that happiness is essential for success, then you need to understand and define happiness. What makes you happy? Why do you sometimes think happy thoughts and other times think thoughts that make you sad, or mad, or scared? What gives you long-term happiness?

Perhaps it seems silly even to discuss happiness. We all know what makes us happy, or at least we think we do. But if we stop to think about happiness, we might realize that *nothing* can make us happy. That is, nothing can make us happy unless we allow it to. Nothing can make us sad, mad, or scared either, unless we allow it to do so. Yet we all relinquish control of our emotions from time to time. We say that someone made us mad, a situation made us scared, or an event made us sad. Hopefully, we can also list the things that seem to make us happy. In reality, the things that get the blame or credit for our emotions are scapegoats for our own choices. Ultimately, we decide (subconsciously) to be mad, sad, scared, or happy.

Do you agree?

🐾 "Life is not always what one wants it to be, but to make the best of it as it is, is the only way of being happy."
—Jennie Jerome Churchill (mother of Winston Churchill)

> "*We all find it challenging to balance our lives and to think positive thoughts continuously. If you have found a way to live without conflict, if harmony and cooperation are basic to all of your actions and interactions, and you are living a life of peace and tranquility, then you must be using a blissful method of thinking, or the proper dosage of a drug like Prozac®, Paxil®, or Zoloft®.*"
>
> —Vetdini ❧

You might find it hard to believe that a boy chooses to be scared when he hears the screeching sound of car tires on the road. It is difficult to think he chooses to be sad when he sees that the car has killed his dog. He doesn't really decide to get mad at the driver and then become angry. His emotions of fear, sadness, and anger are spontaneous. We might all feel similar emotions with the loss of a pet or the sudden death of a loved one. I know I would. But the reason we would feel those emotions is based on the fact that at some time, perhaps years in the past, we made conscious decisions to enter emotional relationships that led up to the natural feelings that seem to be beyond our control. The death of poisonous snake or a serial murderer might evoke completely different feelings because of the choices that we made previously about those lives.

Abraham Lincoln had a favorite view of happiness. He said, "A man is about as happy as he makes up his mind to be." He knew happiness was not something that could be found by searching for it out in the world someplace. Happiness is an inside job. It is neither created nor directly controlled by forces outside of you. Happiness exists only in your mind. You must simply choose to be happy and you will be so.

Happiness has always been important to Americans. The founders of the United States of America believed happiness was as important as life and freedom, yet they never specifically defined happiness. Thomas Jefferson put the following words into the 1776 American Declaration of Independence: "We hold these truths to be self-evident, that all men are created equal, that

❧ "Happiness is when what you think, what you say, and what you do are in harmony."
—Mahatma Gandhi

they are endowed by their Creator with certain unalienable Rights, that among these are Life, Liberty, and the pursuit of Happiness." Once life and liberty were secure, the first Americans wanted to be happy. These were natural rights that all people deserved.

> *Whatever you call the magical guiding force that created us as living, breathing, and thinking creatures—Creator, God, Mother Nature, Holy Spirit, Universal Energy, life-force—let us presume with Jefferson that this divine power gave us not only life but also the desire to live free and to be happy. In essence, we should all be able to function within the limits of universal laws and find pleasure in doing so.*

Jefferson and his colleagues were trying to form a government that Lincoln would later describe as "of the people, by the people, for the people." It would be a nation that would allow all citizens to find their own happiness in their own way. Jefferson and his cohorts declared that all people possess the right to *have* life and the right to *have* liberty, and yet instead of proclaiming that all people have the right to *be* happy, they only argued for the right to *pursue* happiness. Perhaps Jefferson worded the declaration as he did because he believed that the meanings of life and liberty were obvious. On the other hand, happiness was something people had to define and find for themselves.

The idea that happiness is an "inside job" is not just American. At about the same time as the revolution in America, Leo Tolstoy, the Russian novelist and moral philosopher, was writing the book *War and Peace*. One of Tolstoy's writings translates to this, "Man is meant for happiness and happiness is within him." Again, here is a thinker who realized that happiness exists only in a person's mind.

The pursuit of happiness—the search for satisfaction, the quest for tranquility, the race for bliss—sometimes seems more like a curse than an unalienable right. For over two hundred years, Americans have had the right and freedom to pursue happiness; yet we are no happier than George Washington, Alexander Hamilton, Samuel

> *Some pursue happiness. Others create it.* 🐾

🐾 "A happy life consists in tranquility of mind."

—Cicero

Adams, or people of any other era for that matter. If happiness were something we could actually pursue, find, and hold on to, we should all be very happy by now. But modern Americans are no happier than were the members of the Continental Congress.

If we are unable to find and sustain happiness, maybe we are looking for it in the wrong places. Many of us continue to search for it in the future. We say we'll be happy when:

...this day is over.
...the current project is complete.
...the weekend comes.
...school is out.
...we go on vacation.
...we can retire.

It is unrealistic to believe we can be happy all of the time; but if we are not happy now, in this moment, we must ask ourselves why we are not. If we are waiting for something in our lives to change so that we can be happy, we must realize that nothing outside of us needs to change for that to happen. Because our thoughts control our emotions, we simply have to change our thoughts to be happy.

Somewhere along the way, we need to stop pursuing happiness and simply make up our minds to be happy. Indeed, if we are not happy, we have the unalienable right to try to find happiness. However, we will never *be* happy by continually *pursuing* happiness.

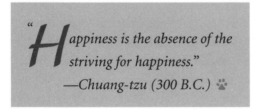

"Happiness is the absence of the striving for happiness."
—Chuang-tzu (300 B.C.)

Life (self-preservation) and liberty (freedom) are natural and can be observed in almost all species of animals. Happiness is similar, yet different. Most animals do not pursue happiness. They know that happiness is not something to go after. They know happiness is not something they can find. Animals just know how to *be happy*. It's simply the way they choose to live. If you could ask the animals of the forests, fields, and

❧ "There is only one happiness in life, to love and be loved."

—George Sand

farms about the meaning of life they would respond, "The purpose of life is to enjoy it."

Aristotle would have agreed with the animals. He held that, "Happiness is the meaning and the purpose of life, the whole aim and end of human existence."

One might find fault with Jefferson's statement, "We hold these truths to be self-evident, that all men are created equal." Look around. We are not all the same. We all have obvious differences. Perhaps "created equal" means that we all came into existence the same. From a biological point of view, we all started out in life about the same way. An egg and sperm got together and formed a zygote that went through mitotic divisions forming an embryo, a fetus, and finally a breathing human being. The biological process is the same for everyone. After people are created, however, things don't stay equal for long. Some children are born into poverty. Some are born with the proverbial silver spoon in their mouths. Some are born with physical features considered to be naturally beautiful while others are born with grotesque disfigurements. Some are male and some are female. Some of us are taller, shorter, faster, darker, or lighter. We obviously aren't equal. Because we don't appear to be equal, we might naturally expect success and happiness to be easier for some than for others.

But appearances are deceiving. The ability to pursue happiness might seem to be different because of ethnic, social, or political heritage, but the opportunity to be happy never changes from the day you are born. Your happiness is dependent upon only one thing: your desire to be happy.

Are most people happy? Take a look around you. Look at your coworkers, colleagues, and customers. Look at the faces of people walking in shopping malls or on the streets. Look at the lips of people standing in checkout lines at grocery, department, or other stores. Look at the people ahead of you or behind you as you stand in lines at theaters. Do most people you see every day appear to be happy?

Take a survey and observe the corners of the mouths of ordinary people. When relaxed, do most people show a frown or a smile? Are the corners of their mouths turned up or down? I have watched thousands of people in airports, business offices, stores, stadiums, factories, and families, as well as in

"Happiness depends upon ourselves."

—Aristotle

my own veterinary clinic. I have been amazed to see how many people look sad most of the time.

> *People choose to have pets for various reasons. People who have lots of problems often adopt a basset hound, simply because it looks as though it has more problems than they do.*

Take a look at the people in an amusement park. Is everyone there happy? Theme parks and carnivals have roller coasters and merry-go-rounds and all sorts of fantasy rides to create pleasure for people. People there should be happy. Why else would people go there other than to be amused and to be made happy? Unfortunately you will observe that some children are cranky and crying, especially toward the end of the day. Some adults will be arguing or disgruntled over lines of people that are too long, refreshments that are too expensive, or other patrons who are rude or pushy. Even in a place where happiness is the main objective, people will find reasons to be mad, sad, or simply unhappy.

Sadness can be found at many other supposedly happy events. Kids cry at the circus because they can't have soda or cotton candy or a pet tiger of their own. At sporting events that are meant for entertainment, adults get mad because players or officials make human mistakes. Parents show their kids that winning is more important than how you play the game. Parents even get violent when their children make errors or fail to perform up to expectations in games that were meant to provide happiness.

Marriages can begin as a lifetime of wedded bliss. But if a wedding day is the happiest day of a person's life, that means things can only get worse from that point on. And things often do. Half of the marriages that were created in harmony and cooperation end with bitter battles in divorce courts. If people could understand happiness, that would not have to happen.

There is hope

Are you one of the millions who go around each day wearing a frown on your face? That may have become your natural look. You are a frowner. It has been said that your face is your own fault after age forty. Think about that, but

🐾 "The happiness of your life depends on the quality of your thoughts."
—Marcus Aurelius

don't worry. Your face can be changed without cosmetics or surgery. By building up the muscles that produce a smile you can, in time, actually turn a frown upside down. Wrinkles can be reduced without a surgical facelift if you exercise the muscles of your forehead, cheeks, and mouth. By building tone in the face muscles that produce a smile, you can actually make the smile become a natural part of your complexion. It costs less than makeup and produces better results than the most expensive plastic surgeon.

> "*To make this planet a happy place, show the world your happy face.*"
>
> —*Vetdini* 🐾

If you want to get along better with other people and look younger and more attractive, the first thing you should put on each morning is a smile. You should do this in the mirror before you brush your teeth or do anything else. Practice smiling. Do it often and with vigor. Build up the facial muscles that make a happy smile. Do it so often that it becomes effortless. Smile a lot. Tone those muscles so that when you meet people later in the day who don't have a smile, you can give them one of yours. Wherever you go you should leave miles of smiles behind you.

We have to acknowledge that not everyone wants to be happy. Some people find great satisfaction in being unhappy. It seems as if some unhappy people want to make more people unhappy so they themselves will feel normal and just like everyone else. While some people light up a room when they enter, unhappy people light up a room by leaving it. I doubt that anyone reading this really wants to be unhappy, so I will assume that you are not in that group; you want to be successful so you can be happy.

Uncovering your own meaning of happiness

Happiness is unique to each individual. Whether or not you are happy depends upon the way you think. No one can make you happy if you choose to be sad. No one can make you happy if you want to be mad. What others do

🐾 "The happiness of a person does not depend upon the absence of conflict, for there will always be some, but in the mastery of conflict resolution."

—Vetdini

may influence your choice to be happy, but what really matters is the answer you give when you ask yourself, "Why am I happy when I am, and how can I be that way more often?"

My definition of happiness may be different from yours. However, the way I discovered my definition might help you define happiness for yourself. As a youth, I liked studying plants and animals. I raised a variety of pets that ranged in size from hamsters to horses. Babies were born, they lived out their lives, and then they died. Some took years to complete their cycle of life. Some took just days. Vegetables and flowers grew in my little corner of the garden from the time my mother let me plant seeds. I always enjoyed watching the cycle of life, from sprouting to blossoming to maturity to the transition back into the earth from where all life originates.

Even as a child studying plants and animals, I wondered about the meaning of life. I thought about what made the life process continue and what made life worthwhile. Like most kids, I wanted to be happy—we all do. I remember being happy most of the time, but not always. I began trying to understand happiness and why I could be so happy one minute and yet sad moments later. I actually started to study happiness from a philosophical and scientific point of view. I read books on happiness written by ancient philosophers, medieval metaphysicians, and modern psychiatrists. I even read the book, *Growing Up Happy,* by Bob Keeshan, a.k.a. Captain Kangaroo.

To learn more about happiness, I went to a man I greatly admired and respected, my grandfather. Surely in his eighty years of experiencing life he had learned the secret of maintaining happiness. He always seemed happy when I was with him. I never saw him fight or argue with anyone. My grandfather was the wisest person I knew, so I asked him, "Gramps, what is happiness?"

First, my grandfather looked at me as if that was the silliest question he had ever heard. But before he could break out laughing, he noticed the serious look in my young eyes. The expression on his elderly face quickly turned to one of contemplation. After a few moments of silence and deep thought, he replied, "Happiness is the simplest of emotions. It comes naturally with the feeling of successful living. If you really want to understand happiness, you should study the animals and note the simplicity of their success and happiness."

❖ "The mere sense of living is joy enough."

—Emily Dickinson

Wow! That sounded like great advice. Thinking that I had just heard the secret to happiness, wisdom handed down from the sages of antiquity, I decided right then and there that I wanted to study animals more closely and chose a career in veterinary medicine and surgery.

Many years later, my parents threw a big party for me when I graduated from Michigan State University as a Doctor of Veterinary Medicine. All of my friends and extended family were there. That included my grandfather, of course. At one point in the festivities, my grandfather took me aside from the merriment and told me, "Grandma and I are simple people. We have been blessed with three wonderful children and many healthy grandchildren. We are very proud of you. When you went off to the university, we weren't sure you would make it. You see, we never thought we would have a doctor in our family." It was then that I learned that *Grampa never intended for me to be a veterinarian*. He simply wanted me to look at the animals and note what naturally made them feel successful and happy.

What I learned from animals about being happy

The first animals I studied in college were dogs. I noticed that dogs seem to be happy with the simplest things in life. They like you to massage their ears, scratch their chests, and rub their bellies. And dogs like to eat. Food seems to make them happy. Treats make them go nuts. Dogs enjoy chasing things like little critters, sticks, balls, and Frisbees. They always make me laugh when they foolishly chase their tails in circles.

The house cats I studied seem to be quite happy when they stretch out purring in the sunshine on a living-room carpet. They also like to have their ears massaged, if they are in the mood. They like to be scratched on their backs just ahead of their tails, and if no one is around to do it for them, they will rub up against just about anything, if they are in the mood. Cats also find great enjoyment in eating and sleeping and chasing things that move, if they are in the mood.

Cows in the pasture seem quite content to have green feed and a comfortable place to ruminate. Horses like to be brushed, to eat oats, and to run in

"We all live with the objective of being happy; our lives are different and yet the same."

—Anne Frank

the field. Even wild animals seem happiest when they are free to search for food and to enjoy their surroundings.

> *The most significant thing animals taught me about happiness is this: To be happy, we must live in the present moment and experience happiness every possible minute of the day.*

I truly believe that animals think the reason they are alive is to enjoy whatever time they may have. They don't waste time worrying about tomorrow or regretting what happened yesterday. They are too busy thinking about today. Whenever they get the chance to be happy, they are.

Worrying makes it difficult to enjoy the present. The advanced human brain allows us to think, but unfortunately it allows us to waste much of our time worrying and regretting. We spend far too much time living in the past or dreading the future rather than being happy in the moment. If we don't have anything to worry about presently, we bring up issues from years ago and fret over what we did or regret what we didn't do.

It is often true that anticipation of a future event can produce happiness—expectation of happiness is happiness itself. Likewise, fear of the future can create unhappy times. Anticipation and fear are just two ways of looking at the future. You can choose either, but the choice seems obvious.

Somewhere along the way, the wisdom of the great Roman orator Seneca has been lost or ignored. It is old but still valid. Two thousand years ago he wrote, "True happiness is to enjoy the present, without anxious dependence upon the future, not to amuse ourselves with either hopes or fears but to rest satisfied with what we have, which is sufficient, for he that is so wants nothing. The great blessings of mankind are within us and within our reach. A wise man is content with his lot, whatever it may be, without wishing for what he has not."

Somewhere along the way, we have complicated the simplicity of happiness. As Andy Rooney put it, "For most of life, nothing wonderful happens. If you don't enjoy getting up and working and finishing your work and sitting down to a meal with family or friends, then the chances are you're not going to be very happy. If someone bases his happiness on major events like a great

---

❖ "The greater part of our happiness or misery depends on our disposition, and not our circumstances."

—Martha Washington

new job, huge amounts of money, a flawlessly happy marriage or a trip to Paris, that person isn't going to be happy much of the time. If on the other hand, happiness depends on a good breakfast, flowers in the yard, a drink, or a nap, then we are more likely to live with quite a bit of happiness."

After years of research and study, these are some of my conclusions regarding happiness:

- The happiest people are those who live in the present. They enjoy every moment possible and create harmony with their existence. Detours along their paths are not problems but rather opportunities to enjoy new scenery.
- The happiest people feel connected with their thoughts of accomplishment. Their dreams, ambitions, efforts, actions, and purposes are congruent.
- The happiest people are not those who are always doing just what they want to do, but doing what they have to do. They are happy in their work and exert themselves to the full extent of their capabilities, and they enjoy it.
- The happiest people are those who are the most appreciative and helpful. They are content with who they are and what they have while striving to improve what they can. They count their blessings more than their cash.
- The happiest people are successful in their own way.

We *can* learn from animals. Pursuing happiness is as foolish as a dog chasing its own tail in circles. Happiness is a part of us and it can be with us wherever we go, if we remember that happiness and success exist only in our thoughts.

Chances are pretty good that if you stop and think about why you want to be successful, it is because you want to be happy. I believe that when it comes to setting goals, the greater happiness comes not from reaching the top, but rather from mastering the technique for getting there with confidence. Collecting the things you want to *have* will give you pleasure, at least for a while. But if you want to find *SMARTER Success*, you need to discover what influences your happiness and then set a goal to *be* happy as often as possible regardless of your circumstances.

"Man's real life is happy, chiefly because he is ever expecting that it soon will be so."
—Edgar Allen Poe

❖ "Who is the happiest of men? He who values the merits of others and in their pleasures takes joy, even as though it were his own."

—Johann von Goethe

❖ "Happiness does not depend upon outward things, but on the way we see them."

—Leo Tolstoy

❖ "It is not the level of prosperity that makes for happiness but the kinship of heart to heart and the way we look at the world. Both attitudes are within the power, so that a man is happy so long as he chooses to be happy, and no one can stop him."

—Aleksander Solzhenitsyn

❖ "The essence of philosophy is that a man should so live that his happiness shall depend as little as possible on external things."

—Epictetus

❖ "The simple truth is that happy people generally don't get sick."

—Bernie S. Siegel, M.D.

❖ "The word happy would lose its meaning if it were not balanced by sadness."

—Carl Jung

❖ "Don't worry. Be happy."

—Bobby McFerrin

❖ "Do not worry; eat three square meals a day; say your prayers; keep your digestion good; exercise; go slow and easy. Maybe there are other things your special case requires to make you happy; but, my friend, these I reckon will give you a good lift."

—Abraham Lincoln

❖ "There is no happiness except in the realization that we have accomplished something."

—Henry Ford

❖ "Serving others is the way to happiness."

—Albert Schweitzer

❖ "Many people have the wrong idea about what constitutes true happiness. It is not attained through self-gratification but through fidelity to a worthy purpose."

—Helen Keller

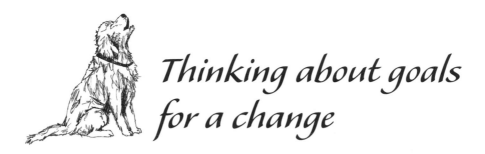

Thinking about goals for a change

Setting any kind of goal implies that you are trying to influence what happens in the future. For your life to be different in the future, it will have to change. But change can be scary because it is accompanied by uncertainty. Therefore, we tend to resist change. Change is neither always good nor always bad. Change does not always create a better life, but all improvement comes from change.

> *By learning why, how, and what type of goals to set, you can influence the future, anticipate change, and minimize the uncertainty in your life.*

Change can be controlled with a great deal of certainty if you take the time to practice a simple trick. It is a trick I learned while working with animals and I use it all the time to influence change. It works like magic. It is simple, but it is not easy. And because it is not easy, very few people use it. With practice and patience, anyone and everyone can learn the trick and influence the future. Unfortunately, few will take the time or expend the effort to do so.

The trick is this: *If you want to control your future, control your thoughts.*

🐾 Two thousand years ago, Marcus Aurelius said, "A man's life is what his thoughts make it."

At first, it might not seem like a trick, but in a way it really is. After all, a magic trick is just a simple act that appears to be supernatural and makes the impossible look real. When analyzed closely, magic can be explained. Even the most fantastic magic tricks are oftentimes very simple illusions. The trick to influencing the future is not supernatural, but it does make reality appear to be an illusion.

By learning the trick to control change and influence the future, you will be able to:

...stop a bad habit like smoking, drinking in excess, or overeating.

...end bad relationships or create new ones that are healthy.

...avoid depression, anxiety, and sleepless nights.

...improve weight, health, and self-confidence.

...relieve pain, stress, and fatigue.

...discover the meaning of life.

...create prosperity.

...live in peace.

...be happy.

If you want to alter events in your future, you simply need to change the way you are thinking. The trick sounds ridiculously simple, but it isn't always easy to change your mind about things. It can be hard mental work to change your way of thinking, especially when you have been thinking a certain way all of your life.

Before you accept or reject the idea that you can control the future by controlling your thoughts, you need to understand one metaphysical concept. Your thoughts create your reality. Everything you believe is real exists only because you believe it exists. Santa Claus is real to a child who believes in him, even though adults know differently. A magician can make a huge elephant disappear from a stage and people believe it happens miraculously right in front of their eyes. To the eyes of the magician's assistants, it is a hoax. Dinosaurs were once real and dominated the earth, if we believe paleontologists. Actually, we have only seen their bones. Some people believe that God created old-looking fossils, which have sparked the imaginations of scientists and artists. It was once believed that only birds could fly; people

   ❊   Buddha taught, "All that we are is the result of what we have thought. What we think, we become."

never would. Now we know differently. People once thought the world was flat; it appears to be round if we believe the pictures we see from space.

W hether or not you think you can control your future by controlling your thoughts, you are right. ❧

The thoughts you think create your beliefs about what is real and what is not. There isn't room here to discuss all the various concepts of reality, but the belief that you create your life with the thoughts you think is as old as history itself. If you grasp this idea, you can create any life you desire. If you don't believe it, that's okay, too.

Can you teach an old dog a new trick?

An intelligent dog of any age will learn a new trick if you show the dog that the new trick is worth learning. The canine associates certain commands, cues, and signals with corresponding behaviors and actions. A smart dog can learn to do a trick if it knows it will get a worthwhile reward like food or attention when the trick is performed. But there is a limit to how much information a dog can handle. Some dogs may have the capacity to learn only a couple of tricks while others can learn many. Because they can learn only a limited number of tricks, occasionally you have to un-teach dogs before they will learn new tricks. Once tricks are well established in the minds of dogs, it is difficult to get them to change. Hence, the expression, "You can't teach an old dog new tricks." Really you can. It just isn't as easy as teaching a young pup.

People are similar in that they sometimes have to un-learn things before they can accept new ideas. If you have lived your lifetime believing that you are helpless and that the future is controlled by fate, it will be challenging to change your mind and take control of your thoughts and future life. If you have always believed that some outside force has complete control over your actions, it will be very difficult to change your way of thinking and take charge of your own thoughts.

❧ Ralph Waldo Emerson wrote, "A man is what he thinks about all day long."

Can you teach an old human being a new trick? Of course, if the person believes the trick is worth learning.

Can you learn to influence the future by changing your way of thinking? Of course, if you are willing to change and accept responsibility for your thoughts.

Perhaps it seems impossible to predict and control events tomorrow, next week, next year, or beyond. To control the events of a lifetime would be unimaginable. A lifetime is a long time. Perhaps it is too much of a task for any one person to control. Even a day or an hour may be too much to control.

Rather than trying to control vast amounts of time like a whole life, a day, or an hour, perhaps you can start by trying to control a very short period of time. The smallest unit of time in anyone's life is a thought. A thought is such a short increment of time and passes so quickly that it cannot be measured on a clock. A thought travels through your mind in less than a nanosecond. It is faster than a speeding bullet or the blink of an eye.

What constitutes a thought? Well, I am not sure, but I do know this:

- An individual thought is extremely small and exists for only a very short period of time. A thought can enter your mind and exit in a flash.
- Thoughts accumulate into moments. Moments add up and are measured with minutes, days, and then years that make up a lifetime.
- Although thoughts are small, you cannot consciously think more than one thought at a time. You can switch from one thought to another to another incredibly fast, but no two thoughts can occupy the central processing center in your brain at the same time. You cannot consciously think about the image of a horse and the image of a dog simultaneously. You can switch back and forth between the two images so incredibly fast that it seems as if you are thinking about them both simultaneously, but the individual thoughts about the images are processed one at a time.
- No one else can control your thoughts—unless, of course, you let them.
- You can control your own individual thoughts, if you want to.
- You can't control the thought of any other person, unless they let you.

❧ James Lane Allen declared, "A man is literally what he thinks." "Dream lofty dreams and as you dream so shall you become. Your vision is the promise of what you one day will be. Your idea is the prophecy of what you shall at last unveil."

- You can't control any thoughts that were processed yesterday. Today, you can't control the thoughts you might have in the distant future. You can only control the individual thought you have right now.
- The thought that you are currently processing at the speed of light will be replaced by a new thought. It is that new thought that is the most important. How you choose your next thought is the basis for your future thinking.

Scientists tell us we think over sixty thousand thoughts per day. Wow! That's a lot of thinking. I am not sure who counted all of those thoughts but I am impressed that someone would take the time to do so. Many of the thoughts we think are repetitive, some are spin-offs of other thoughts, and some may even be original. New, borrowed, or stolen, the ideas we think are our own; and we control which ones we process and which ones we store or reject.

Every thought you think counts. Once you process a thought, it goes into your brain's thought storage area, which we call memory. When you want to remember something, your brain goes to the thought storage area and recalls a thought. If you process happy, healthy thoughts most of the time, then there will be more happy, healthy thoughts from which your brain can choose when you need to remember something. Your recall will naturally be healthy and happy most of the time. If your thoughts are usually depressing, negative thoughts, then your brain will have mostly negative thoughts to recall and your memory and thinking will be mostly negative.

Your future, your personal character, and all of your actions begin with a single thought. If you continually think new thoughts that are happy, and then store those happy thoughts, everything you remember in the future will be good, healthy, and happy. That may not be realistic, but if it were possible, it could make a very positive impact on your future.

Controlling one individual thought seems manageable. With a little effort, you can think whatever you like. If you think a happy thought, and then one more, you can link many happy thoughts together, one after another, thereby creating a long and happy life filled with healthy thoughts. It all begins with controlling the thought you are about to think.

🐾 Viktor Frankl studied human behavior in a Nazi concentration camp where he noted that, "Man does not simply exist, but always decides what his existence will be, what he will become in the next moment."

It seems as though anyone should be able to do something as simple as controlling an individual thought. And of course we can, but we don't. We allow other people to tell us what to think. We permit people to tell us what we want to have. We let others determine what will make us happy. We relinquish control of our thinking and of our destinies by allowing people to control our present and future thoughts.

As children, parents tell us what to think. As students, teachers tell us what to think. As friends, peers tell us what to think. As members of religious groups, clergy tell us what to think. As constituents, politicians tell us what to think. As employees, employers tell us what to think. As consumers, advertisements tell us what to think. People around us are constantly telling us what to think. We are so used to people telling us what to think that we don't realize how much control we have given up to outside influences.

If we could hear ourselves speak, we might realize how often we give up control of our thoughts. Listen to yourself the next time you say, "The accident made me scared." "The death made me sad." "She made me mad." In essence, every time we state that anything made us feel or think a certain way, we are saying that outside forces controlled our thoughts. People and events cannot make us feel mad, glad, sad, or scared, unless we let them.

Unless you give up your unalienable rights, no one can control your emotions and feelings. By taking control of your own thinking and by choosing your individual thoughts carefully, you can have tremendous influence on your future.

Lifetime goals are accomplished by breaking them down into yearly goals. Yearly goals can be broken down into monthly or weekly goals. These goals can be broken down into daily goals. Daily goals can be broken down into smaller and smaller goals. Eventually, goals for a lifetime, a year, a month, a day, or a moment can be broken down to goals for a thought. Therefore, lifetime goals are dependent upon the goals you set for your next thought.

Simultaneous thought processing and the subconscious

While you are reading this, you undoubtedly are thinking many thoughts. Perhaps you find these ideas intriguing. Perhaps you disagree. Perhaps you don't fully understand how you can be thinking about many things and yet

❧ Earl Nightingale was a modern thinker who based his ideas on volumes of literature and observed that, "The strangest secret in life is: We become what we think about."

think only one thought at a time. All these thoughts are flowing through your mind at incredible speed, making them seem as if they are being thought about all at the same time.

Although you think only one thought at a time, many thoughts are being processed in your head simultaneously. Parts of your brain function behind the scenes to regulate your body's homeostasis—metabolism, defense systems, temperature, and other factors involved in the maintenance of your body. Parts of your brain specialize in interpreting the senses of touch, sight, hearing, taste, and smell. Many of these areas are functioning continuously without your conscious awareness. They are controlled by subconscious thoughts. Subconscious thoughts go on constantly without your effort. For the most part they take care of themselves. There are things you can do to alter subconscious thoughts, but thoughts involving homeostasis are not changed as easily as conscious thoughts.

The conscious thoughts that you can think one at a time are the ones you control by allowing them into your higher thought center. You and I alone choose to think these thoughts.

Some conscious thoughts are chained together, repeating themselves over and over again, almost as though they were subconscious. These individual thoughts create your individual way of thinking about things like politics, religion, and moral values. Some thoughts jump into your conscious thought-processing center from your memory center instantaneously when other thoughts are processed. Even though you don't always know where thoughts originate, you can control whether or not they stay in your thinking.

> "*If you are to become what you have desired, a significant change may be required.*"
> —*Vetdini* ❖

If you want to set goals to take control of your own destiny and to make significant changes in your life, you may have to make significant changes in your thinking processes. If you are willing to change your way of thinking, you can create a happier and healthier life for yourself and for those whose health and happiness depend upon you.

❖ "Change your thoughts and you can change the world."

—Norman Vincent Peale

Actually, your thinking is always changing. Change is inevitable. You don't have a choice. Everything changes. You will change. Babies are born and people die. Relationships develop, alter, and end. Friends and colleagues change. Technology changes. Jobs come and go. The important issue is not whether or not you will change, but rather, how much control will you have over that change?

> *It has been said that the only place there is no change is in the cemetery. But that is not really true. Embalming with chemical preservatives slows the decaying process, but change occurs even in the grave.*

The British naturalist Charles Darwin studied and lectured on the evolution of animal species. He observed, "It is not the strongest of the species that survive, nor the most intelligent, but the ones most responsive to change." You don't have to let change be a matter of chance. You can make it a matter of choice. It starts with choosing your own thoughts. You don't have to let change be something you wait for if you make it something you work for. Instead of spending time wishing, you can spend your time working. Sometimes change takes work. Don't be like the boy who lay in the pasture waiting for a cow to pass over and give him a drink of milk. Cows don't give milk. You have to take it from them.

It is a significant moment in your life when you realize that you may not be able to control what happens around you, or what happens to you, but you can control what happens in you. Because you cannot control others (unless you use force or have their permission) and you can control your own life (unless you give up your freedom to do so), your greatest opportunity to control the future is by setting goals for yourself. The British writer, Aldous Huxley, said after years of studying and experiencing life, "I wanted to change the world. But I have found that the only thing one can be sure of changing is oneself." By concentrating on changing yourself, you will find that the people and events around you will change, oftentimes in

---

❧ "If you want to change the world, start by controlling what you can. Your number one asset is the control you have over your own life. To change the world, start by changing your own thoughts."

—Leo Tolstoy

a similar way. If we are to change humanity, we must begin by changing ourselves.

If you believe thoughts make up your life and if you believe you can control your thoughts, one thought after another, then you should be able to continue to do

> " *T*he thoughts we think create our reality. Together we can change the world—one thought at a time."
> —Vetdini 🐾

that day after day. And once you can control your thoughts on a regular basis, you will have substantial and meaningful control over your life.

🐾 "We must be the change we wish to see in the world."

—Mahatma Gandhi

🐾 "Life is not a static thing. The only people who do not change their minds are incompetents in asylums, and those in cemeteries."

—Everett M. Dirksen

🐾 "We choose our joys and sorrows long before we experience them."

—Kahlil Gibran

🐾 "He who cannot change the very fabric of his thoughts will never be able to change reality."

—Anwar Sadat

Why set goals

More than eighty percent of the people with whom I talk about goals tell me they have no goals. Do you have positive goals for your life? Perhaps you do and don't realize it. The English language is rich with words that have meanings and definitions similar to the word "goal." Maybe you don't think you have goals. Perhaps, instead, you have dreams, objectives, targets, future plans, destinations, finish lines, aims, aspirations, expectations, visions, fantasies, or wishes. These all carry subtle differences in meaning or connotation but are considered to be the same or very similar in the context of this discussion. A goal by any other name can give you the same direction for changing your life.

A professional speaker and friend of mine, Jeff Staads, lectures to groups on the subject of goal-setting. In his goal-setting program, "When Dreams Become Reality," he asks members of his audience, "What did you want to be when you grew up?" Followed

> *"If change is what you desire, different goals you must acquire."*
> —*Vetdini* 🐾

by, "How many of you are doing that right now?" Jeff tells me that less than one percent are doing what they wanted to do, unless he is speaking to nurses. He has found that many nurses wanted to be nurses at an early age. Jeff wanted to be a fireman. Other kids with whom he grew up wanted to be astronauts, cowboys, movie stars, or baseball players. He said that in all of his years of professional speaking, he has never met anyone who said they wanted to grow up to be an accountant, middle manager, sales clerk, or a professional speaker.

Professional speakers like Jeff Staads can relate countless stories of people whom they inspired to pursue childhood dreams after they had entered adulthood. Jeff outlines a course of action one can take to make dreams come true. He helps people realize that they can have and be what they desire if they take the time and effort to create a plan and carry it out.

A goal is more than just a whim. It is something you really, really want. To have a clear, attainable goal, you must be able to define it well. It must be something you can write down on paper. Writing out a goal makes it tangible—something you can see. A written goal makes your idea become more than just a fleeting wish. A goal is a personal desire for change to which you have given serious thought. Goals should make you stretch.

> " *. . . a man's reach should exceed his grasp, or what's a heaven for?"*
> —Robert Browning

You need to set goals if you want to control the change that occurs in your life. To control change, you simply control the thoughts that you are thinking. To control your thoughts, you need to learn as much as you can about the source of your thoughts. It may appear that your parents or children or siblings or spouse or colleagues or even your enemies are responsible for putting thoughts in your head. However, only you can control whether they stay.

Goals can make the difference between having a mediocre existence or enjoying a memorable life. The man who created one of America's greatest department store chains knew that goals make a great difference in a person's life. J.C. Penney said, "Give me a stock clerk with a goal and I'll give you a man who will make history. Give me a man without a goal and I'll give you a stock clerk."

Remember that to go forward with no aim or destination in mind is non-directional. Without a direction you will have a very uncertain future. Having no goals in life is like living as a homeless homing pigeon. The bird flies and eats and lives, but continually wanders, never finding its way home.

Do animals have goals?

When a robin begins to build a nest, it instinctively knows what it is creating. Somewhere within its mind is a blueprint inherited from its ancestors. Like other birds, the robin has a pretty good idea of where a nest should be located. The bird knows how wide to make it and how high to build the sides of the nest. It chooses building materials that will create a home suitable for laying and hatching eggs. The dimensions will be adequate for raising chicks. The robin naturally knows how, why, when, and where to build a nest. It knows all this by instinct.

When a fox chases a rabbit, it does so because it knows it must eat to survive. Foxes don't eat stones or dirt or sticks for nutrition. They eat and digest meat because they are foxes and that is what foxes do. Behaviors that assure survival are natural to animals. They survive by using their instincts.

A female dog in heat knows it needs a male to get pregnant, have puppies, and propagate the species. Dogs will travel miles to do what is necessary to start a family. The pheromones that female dogs release to attract mates and how they react to other dogs are part of their nature. They naturally do what dogs do to make sure the canine family continues generation after generation. Animals reproduce by instinct.

We could say that animals have subconscious goals to find shelter and food and to reproduce. However, goals like these do not originate from an animal's own thinking. They are simple instincts. Few animals, other than humans, have the ability to create and reach goals that are more than instinctive. Goals are human luxuries that allow us to plan for improvement in our lives and in our surroundings. Goals differentiate us from other animals as well as from other humans.

Goals are created from desire

Two strong opposing emotions, fear and desire, are the major influences on our thoughts and the actions those thoughts produce. They motivate us to do almost everything. You can probably think of hundreds of other reasons that cause people to think and act, but all of those reasons can be categorized under these two basic emotions. When you boil down what motivates people, fear and desire are the basic reasons we do everything we do.

Fear makes us run away from things we don't want in our lives. Fear is a reaction that motivates us to avoid situations. In other words, fear establishes a negative goal, which is not really a goal at all. Fear tells us what to evade but does not give us direction or a destination to move toward. Fear injects pessimism, hopelessness, and helplessness into our thinking.

Fear is a very powerful motivator that may develop from actual experience or from simply hearing or seeing scary events. It can begin when we are very young and last a lifetime. Fear can be learned and also can be unlearned through counseling and therapy. Most fears can be overcome with the power of positive desire, if the desire is great enough.

The opposite of fear is desire. Desire drives us toward something that we want to have in life. Desire can be a positive, active motivator that keeps us moving toward our goal. It sets a destination. Although we may never reach our goal, we can at least establish a positive direction in our lives. Desire instills hope, optimism, and enthusiasm into our thoughts about the future.

> *Desire determines direction.*
> *Direction determines destiny.*

A goal is created because you desire an outcome rather than fear a consequence. Setting a goal is the positive and proactive way to create and control your future by giving you direction.

What creates desire?

Need motivates us to satisfy the basics in life like food, shelter, and love. Instincts drive animals to reach for what they need. *Want* motivates us to reach for more.

Around the middle of the twentieth century, a psychologist by the name of Abraham Maslow carried out extensive research in the area of motivation. He wanted to uncover the reasons people did what they did. He categorized the reasons people do things into progressive levels, which he called a hierarchy of needs. Maslow categorized the sources of motivation in the following way, extending from the most basic to the highest level:

1. Physiological
2. Safety/security
3. Belongingness and love

4. Esteem
5. Cognitive (knowledge)
6. Aesthetic (beauty)
7. Self-actualization (fulfillment)
8. Transcendence (exceed human limitations)

Although Maslow's ideas were published over fifty years ago and may lack scientific evidence to support the hierarchy, they have become some of the most popular and most often quoted theories of human motivation. Not everyone is motivated in the order of Maslow's list and each level may have subgroups, but he did give us a model for studying why we do what we do.

The less complex creatures in the animal world instinctively strive for two goals from the most basic levels: survival and reproduction. Although those two goals are essential for most humans as well, our species is different. We have the capability to set and to reach for goals far more complex than just staying alive and ensuring the continuation of our kind. We can establish goals that not only meet our basic needs but also fulfill our (sometimes) frivolous desires. We can dream of what could be and then establish goals to make that happen. We can attain ends that far exceed what Maslow referred to as basic needs.

> *Caution! When we reach for more than we really need, we risk letting desire convert into greed.*

There are three phases of human motivation:

1. People do things because they have to. A child goes to school because of a parent's force or influence. An adult works at a job in exchange for food and housing or because of social pressure.
2. People do things because they feel a need. A child realizes that education will open doors to opportunities in the future. School is still a chore, but parental influence or force is not required. An adult goes to work knowing that the job will provide a paycheck that will allow for the purchase of things that will make life better.
3. People do things because they want to. A child genuinely likes to go to school. An adult likes to work at a job that is fulfilling and rewarding.

When we get to the point that we do things because we want to, we can set goals to create the future we desire. When we feel we have to or need to do something, we are pursuing the goals of someone else. In the third phase, when we *want* to do what we are doing, we can freely go after our own dreams.

Many people never have desires beyond their basic needs and never really think about or establish their own goals. That's okay if you just want to go along with the crowd. However, going along with the pack is not always the best plan for a happy and healthy life. You might think you are following a good leader, when you are actually following a follower who doesn't know the right way, either.

Have you heard the legends of the lemmings? Lemmings are fuzzy little creatures of Scandinavian lore that can teach us a lesson. Folktales suggest that each of these wild mouse-like creatures will follow the one in front of it so closely and intently that packs of them will jump off high cliffs and fall to their deaths, hundreds at a time. The lemmings in the front of the pack cannot hold the others back, who just keep going forward, pushing the ones ahead of them. They commit mass suicide. We can learn from the lemmings that following the crowd is not always the wisest or safest way to go.

> *Hundreds of excuses can be reasoned for why you can't do something, when all you need is one good reason why you can.* 🐾

Occasionally people will stumble upon Truth—the path they know is right—but most of the time they catch their balance and continue on following the majority. It seems simple, but it isn't very easy to set your own goals, break from the pack, and plan your own journey. Peer pressure is powerful. It is easier to flow with the status quo. But when you are certain you know what you want, that certainty can give you the strength to do what is right. When you know what you want and why you want it, you will feel confident to break away from the crowd and pursue your own personal destination.

The wisdom of a cat

Perhaps animals don't really set goals as humans do, but we can still learn about goals from animals. A talking cat once asked a lost little girl named Alice, "Where are you going?"

Alice looked at the roads she could choose to take, thought for a moment, and then replied, "Nowhere in particular."

The cat then displayed uncanny feline wisdom by explaining, "If your goal is to get to nowhere, then any road will get you there."

The cat seemed to know that without a destination, it doesn't matter which road you take or which way you go. Destinations are important because they establish your direction and ultimately define your life. Where you are going is significant, but not nearly as important as the path you choose to get there. It seems so obvious that all of us should know where we are going. We should have goals and desires for where we want to go, but sadly, most of us don't.

Navigating the waters

Some people live their lives as if they were empty bottles bobbing along in the river of life. They drift aimlessly, with little or no control over their course. The bottles are susceptible to winds and waves, tides, and currents. Eventually, the bottles may wash ashore or they may just float aimlessly about for a lifetime. There is nothing wrong with drifting, if that is your desire and you realize you are allowing it to happen.

But you don't have to be a floater. You can make your life more like a boat than a bottle. When a boat has some method of steering, like a rudder, paddles, or adjustable propulsion, you can control its direction. With a little navigation, you can adjust your direction so you can reach or avoid any destination. Unlike a floating bottle, you have the ability to increase or decrease your speed and move toward any destination you desire.

Sometimes you might feel as if you are living life in a sailboat. You can steer the vessel, but you can't possibly reach your goal because the wind is in your face. Unlike mechanically powered boats, a sailboat cannot sail directly into the wind and that can make a goal look impossible to reach. However, if a skipper knows how to traverse the wind and tack back and forth across the wind, the boat eventually will end up at a destination that was originally directly into the wind. After all, the same wind that blows a ship into port can push another out into open water. Like the wind, the forces that motivate you to move need not determine your direction or your speed.

> *A pessimist complains about the wind.*
> *An optimist expects it to change.*
> *A realist adjusts the sails.*

For generations, sailors thought that sailboats could travel at velocities no faster than the wind. Therefore, early sailing vessels with their open billowing sails were limited by the speed of the wind. Somewhere along the way, sailors learned that by holding the sail at an angle, the wind was forced to travel faster around the front of the sail than the back. This created a force similar to the lift produced by a wing that allows a bird or an airplane to fly. The boat was actually pulled into the wind and could travel forward faster than the wind. At one time in history this seemed impossible. Now we take it for granted. Even though you cannot control the direction or force of the winds in your life, you can set your own sails and determine your direction.

For years I refused to set goals in my life because I was afraid of failing to reach them. I was afraid that people would make fun of me if I did not reach my goals. So if I didn't set goals, I couldn't fail, and people would not be derisive. Therefore, I didn't take risks.

> *The greatest hazard in life is to risk nothing.* 🐾

Somewhere along the way, I learned that avoiding failure does not ensure success. Setting a goal meant taking the risk of failing to reach that goal, but everything I did incurred risks. I realized that all of my animal patients were constantly taking risks. Simply living incurred the risk of dying. To attempt to treat a seriously sick animal was to risk losing a patient, but to refuse the attempt was to ensure death. To try was to risk failure, but risks had to be taken. Goals had to be set, even if they were never reached.

People who risk nothing, do nothing. They may elude suffering and sorrow, but they also avoid changing, learning, feeling, and communicating. Chained by fear of failure, they relinquish their freedom and become slaves to those who take risks. We need to accept the risk of failure and try. We need to set a course and then progress toward it.

That isn't to say that you have to be headed somewhere all the time. You don't always have to be moving. Rest and relaxation are important, too. There will be times when you are still or when progress is not evident, and that is okay. It is good to take a break, rest, and regenerate your spirits. If you stand still, let it be a conscious decision. Once you are rested and ready to go again, you shouldn't let the lack of wind stop your advancement. Remember the old saying translated from Latin, "If there is no wind, row." It often takes personal energy and work to get where you want to go.

You can set goals in any area of your life that you want to influence or try to control. You can set goals for your relationships with friends and family members. You can develop financial goals, professional goals, or community goals. You can establish goals for your religious life. You can plan goals in some areas of your life and not in others. You can give direction to your life—as much or as little as you choose. Goals will help you attain *SMARTER Success.*

How to set goals

M any analogies can be used to explain how to set goals. You might compare goal setting to planning a trip. You could use a map as simple as a line drawing to help you get from where you are to where you want to be. Or you might use a complex highway map that shows details of intersections, railroad crossings, points of interest, and attractions along the way. Aviation and relief maps could show you the hills and valleys, mountains and prairies. If you plot your life as you would a trip on a map, you will need to plan for fuel (energy and motivation) along the way, and rest stops (short breaks or vacations). When the trip is well planned, the map will describe the course you should follow to get to your goal.

You might visualize your goal at the top of a ladder—a step-by-step approach. You can work on taking one step at a time until you get to the top. Each rung of the ladder should be well described with directions to the next level that will get you closer to your ultimate goal. You will need energy every step of the way. You may want to prearrange little boosts of support from your family and friends when you will need to get to the next rung.

Goal setting can be compared to a ring of keys. Keys can unlock doors and the potential within you. People along the way will want to sell you the keys to your success. Be aware of charlatans and unscrupulous vendors, as many keys will not fit your specific needs. It is up to you to find the keys that will unlock your own potential and help you reach your goals. Sometimes it only takes one key to open the secret door that presents you with your goal. Such keys often come with a high price that you must pay with money, time and energy.

Goal setting can be compared to baking a cake, which is not as easy as it looks. Anyone can create a cake by just putting ingredients into a pan and then baking them in an oven for half an hour. Technically, a cake will be produced. However, it might not be edible or look like anything ever seen before. If you want to make a cake that tastes good and looks great, you will need to do much more than just assemble and cook the ingredients. Anyone with experience in baking cakes can tell you that there are certain steps you must take to bake a cake that is delicious and pleasing to the eye.

First, you need to develop the idea to bake a cake. Clearly envision your cake. Will it be a flat sheet cake or a layered cake? Round, square, or a special shape? What flavor will it be? How large will it be? Will it have frosting? What flavor or color will you choose for the frosting?

Once you have the idea in your head you will need a recipe. A recipe is more than just a list of ingredients that must be purchased or gathered together. It also tells you in what order the ingredients should be added, folded, or blended in a bowl. Mixing the wrong proportions or in the wrong order can make a mess. (I learned that from experience.) Next you will need to transfer the mixture to a pan or something to hold the ingredients together until the batter becomes firm. You will need to know if the pan should be greased or not greased. The recipe will also tell you how long to bake the cake and at what temperature. You will even have to know how to cool the cake properly. Baking a cake is simple but not easy, unless you know what you are doing.

Goal setting is just as simple as baking a cake. But like so many other things, it is not easy unless you know not only *what* to do but also *how* to do it. A recipe for success can make it less difficult. You can use recipes that come from people who previously accomplished similar goals, or you can create one from personal experience. By learning a technique, then following the system and practicing it, both goal setting and cake baking can become easy.

Knowing how to do something is essential in the kitchen, in goal setting, and in the veterinary profession. Veterinary schools train people to help animals, but sometimes graduates don't know how to implement what they know needs to be done. A short story about one of my tiger patients will help illustrate this point.

A tale of a tiger's toe

I was asked to look at a Siberian tiger with a sore foot. Because of its size, the owner could not bring the cat to my clinic, so I went to the tiger. When I arrived at the little zoo where he lived, I found the tiger reclining in the sun on a rock perch alongside the fence of his outdoor exercise area. I estimated his weight to be about five hundred pounds, which was a bit more cat than you could handle just by holding the scruff of his neck. The big cat let me get within inches of him for an examination if I remained quiet and calm. As I got closer to him, I could see the source of his pain and the cause of his problem. One of his toenails had grown very long and had curled around into the soft pad on the bottom of his foot. The area was red and inflamed and looked infected.

> Long toenails are common in animals. Some animals don't wear their nails down naturally and need to have them trimmed occasionally. If an animal's nails are not trimmed and if there is no friction on the nail when the animal walks, the nail can grow quite long. Sometimes the nail grows in a curl, and if it doesn't hit the skin or pad of the foot it can actually form a ring and grow in loops indefinitely.

I could see that the tiger's other toenails were just fine. Something must have gone wrong with the one toenail to make it grow irregularly. Whatever the reason for the long nail, my diagnosis and treatment were simple: cut the toenail off at a point where it would no longer cause pain when the tiger walked. It was a simple idea but not an easy task on a very large cat.

I knew from experience that the tiger was not going to hold out his paw for a pedicure. I also knew that he was far too big for anyone to hold securely so I could enter his cage. I could wait until he fell asleep and then sneak up and clip the nail off, but cats are light sleepers with quick reflexes. If I did nothing, the nail might fall off by itself, but the tiger might be lame for a very long time. The infection could spread up though his foot or turn into gangrene and become life-threatening. Something needed to be done. I knew what to do. That was simple—the tiger needed a toenail trimmed. How to accomplish the task was another issue.

The only thing I could do that made sense was to give the tiger a sedative. If I knocked him out I could go in and trim the nail in no time. Again, that sounds simple. It even looks easy when they do it in the nature shows on television. However, anesthetizing a large cat can be tricky. The amount of sedative drug needed is determined according to the animal's weight. This tiger was not about to step on a scale; I had to guess his weight. All the drug dosages available in my books describe the amount of drug to use in normal, healthy animals. This tiger was neither completely normal nor totally healthy. If this tiger had a fever from the infection in his foot, that could change the way he recovered from the sedative. He didn't want any part of a thermometer put in his mouth, his ear, or under his tail, so taking a body temperature was out of the question. Although the animal looked healthy from a distance, I was unable to give him a physical examination before anesthesia, as I would have liked.

Another issue was administration of the drug. It had to be injected properly. A shot in the muscle would have worked well, but getting the injection into the muscle—not just under the skin and not into bone, lungs, or intestines—could be challenging. A dart gun might work, but even at close range the rifle might shoot the medicine into the wrong place. The wrong dosage or an improper injection could produce a fatal result.

My goal was to help the tiger without adding to his pain and suffering. Therefore, I gave the situation careful consideration before doing anything. Whatever I would do with a cat this size involved risk, both for the patient and myself. Doing nothing meant certain suffering for the tiger. I had to try to help the animal, but I needed to minimize the risk for us all.

To minimize the risk to the patient, I used about half the dosage of sedative drug that is usually given to big cats. I have put many cats down before and know that the bigger cats need surprisingly little of the same drug I use on smaller patients. I loaded my syringe with only three times the amount of sedative I would use on a ten-pound kitty. I planned to inject that small dose into a tiger that weighed fifty times as much.

Because the tiger was not afraid of me, I had an assistant draw his attention to the other side of the cage while I walked up to the fence. With a small syringe in my hand, I reached through the fence and gave the tiger a quick poke in the muscle of his back leg. The startled tiger quickly jumped off his perch and turned toward me. He started walking directly toward me while I stood as still as a statue. He got closer and closer to the fence where I was standing. Admittedly, I was a little nervous. Then he rubbed his face against the fence and almost started to purr. He didn't realize what I had done, or if he did, he forgave me and now wanted me to scratch his ears. I talked to him in a soft, comforting voice, but I kept my hands to myself.

In a few minutes, he lay down. With an emergency escape route established beforehand, I entered his cage, cut the toenail off at the quick, treated his sore footpad with iodine, and got out of his lair. His owner later told me that he got up and walked around within a few hours after I left the zoo. Three days later he was back to normal and walked without a limp.

Prior to pursuing any goal, good judgment must be applied to the possible ways it can be accomplished. The methods you use to reach your goals are as important as the goals themselves. Some people desire to realize their dreams so much that they will do anything to make them come true. They covet things so badly that they will lie, steal, or even kill in order to get what they want. Some people will give up priceless possessions to purchase things they hope will make them happy. They sacrifice families and friends for finances and careers. They forfeit their personal integrity to attain political power or social influence. These losses are unnecessary if you give your goals appropriate consideration and know what you are after and how to get what you really want.

Somewhere along the way you need to realize that even though a goal looks simple, like cutting a toenail, the most obvious way to reach the goal is not always the best. Knowledge and experience can make the goal less formidable. Simple goals that look complicated, impossible, or extremely risky can be reached with confidence. The more you know about your goals and how others have failed and succeeded in reaching similar goals, the better you will be able to accomplish your dreams without losing what you already have.

The process of setting and reaching for goals is like working with tigers and baking cakes in the kitchen. Tasks might seem simple, but they get complicated if you don't know what you are doing. The more information you can gather, the more likely you are to achieve your dreams. Even seemingly impossible goals can be accomplished if you learn more about them. Before you reject the possibilities, you need to explore the ways others have reached similar goals. By learning where others have stumbled or failed, you can avoid common pitfalls and progress steadily toward your goals.

Set and reach for goals with clarity, strategy, and action

After you have clearly developed goals worthy of your efforts, you can take the next step and formulate a plan to continue your journey. Here are ten ideas you can use to help you set and reach goals:

1. Write out goals.
2. Hide goals and seek support.
3. Unify goals.
4. Make commitments.
5. List benefits.
6. Prioritize goals.
7. Uncover necessary knowledge.
8. Take action.
9. List obstacles and plan strategies to overcome them.
10. Review goals and success often.

1. Write out goals

If a goal is important, you should write it out in clear and concise detail. Writing out goals changes them from transient thoughts to documented ideas that are almost tangible. Written goals can be seen, reviewed, and revised, which increases effectiveness and efficiency.

An old Chinese proverb says that the palest ink is better than the best memory. Perhaps you always remember everything you want to do, but can you remember everything you are *supposed to do*? A list, even just a few scribbles on a piece of paper, can help assure that you don't forget important things. You think so many thoughts in continuous succession that some of them naturally slip out of your memory. To avoid forgetting important things, like goals, you need to write them down. For some special goals, there are other means of reminding you of what is important.

If you are like me, you constantly depend upon reminders. In your home, bells remind you to remove food from the microwave, take a cake out of the oven, or pull clothes from the dryer. In your car, buzzers remind you to fasten your seat belt, remove your keys, fill the tank with fuel, and close the door. Alarm clocks and watches remind you to wake up, take medication, and complete timely tasks. You use techno-gadgets to remind you to do things all the time.

A portrait of a spouse, significant other, children, parents, or pets can remind you of why you are doing what you are doing. Perhaps a simple picture can motivate you to go to work, clean the house, cook dinner, or care for the family. A photo of a home or a car can remind you of your dreams to own such things. A ring on your finger can remind you of a commitment and the goal you have to keep that commitment. Post-it notes, calendars, electronic notebooks, and organizers can refresh your memory and remind you of goals.

You may not have written goals for your religious or spiritual objectives, but many people wear a piece of jewelry or clothing to remind them and others of their faith. Religious groups have their own unique symbols that represent spiritual goals. A cross or crucifix, a bindi (a colored dot on the forehead), the Star of David, a cap, turban, or other covering for the head, and the sign of a fish are all symbols that remind people of religious convictions, values, and goals.

You have a lot to remember. Written goals are a great way to remind yourself of the direction you desire to go when you become focused and busy handling other details of your life. The simple act of writing things down—especially things like goals—can help reinforce them as well as remind you of them.

As you organize your goals, you can make separate lists of short-term goals, mid-range goals, and long-term goals. Several time-management planners have various ways to create lists that work very well. A small spiral notebook can also be helpful. Some goals you will want to accomplish yet today. Some goals will be for tomorrow. Some goals will be created to accomplish over your lifetime. Your goal recording system can be as complicated or as simple as you like.

> *Perhaps there is someone, often a spouse, who makes "honey-do" lists for you. That's okay for accomplishing the goals of others, but a list you make for yourself is more gratifying, unless, of course, your primary goal is to keep that someone happy.*

Lists are essential when you have many important things to remember. Airplane pilots have so many things to do before takeoff that they rely on lists. They must verify that all the switches and gauges and buttons and knobs and motors and radios and controls are working properly. A pilot might be able to tell at a glance that all the systems are set and functioning properly, but even the veteran pilot cannot depend solely upon memory. Personally, I would rather fly in a plane with a competent rookie pilot who used a pre-flight checklist than board a plane flown by an ace pilot who did not. There are just too many things to remember.

A checklist is just as important for the pilot of a life as it is for the pilot of a plane. If your life is as important to you as the airplane is to the pilot, perhaps you should also consider using a checklist.

A checklist or a "To Do List" is a great tool to use for accomplishing goals in the near future. I like to make a list of things to do every day. I start the list before I go to bed at night and then I can sleep without trying to remember or worry about what I have to do tomorrow.

2. Hide goals and seek support

Disclosing your goals sometimes makes your journey more difficult. Goals can produce jealousy and rivalry. Competitors may want you to fail. Therefore, you should hide your written goals from those who might hinder your plans. You can secure your written goals in a wallet, purse, personal time-management organizer, dresser drawer, holy book, or other sacred place. Conceal your goals from people who might prevent you from accomplishing your dreams.

Another reason to conceal your goals is because your ego can easily get involved in goal setting. By flaunting your goals you may be trying to impress people with your potential, thereby improving your self-image. This is a weak form of boasting that seldom accomplishes the intent.

On the other hand, you will need to share your goals with those whose help and support you will need. You can delegate tasks to other people who will share in your rewards. You can collaborate with those who have similar goals. You might be able to work together more efficiently than separately.

> *The foundation of your accomplishments and the success you enjoy are built on the contributions of many others. Successful people are looked up to because they are standing on the shoulders of giants.*

If you must concentrate your efforts on one particular goal for a period of time, you should let the people involved in other goals know that you have not abandoned them. Keep others abreast of your progress and remind them that by working to accomplish different goals, you still support their goals. For example, children need to know that while you are building a business, the business will help the family by providing money and opportunities that would otherwise be unavailable.

3. Unify goals

In a very simple life, a solitary goal might suffice. But unless one lives in a monastery, on a deserted island, or in social seclusion, life is far from simple. You have many needs, wants, and desires. Therefore, you naturally create multiple goals, dreams, and wishes.

Because you cannot head in different directions toward two goals at the same time, it is important to establish goals that complement each other and are unified. When you are moving toward your professional or financial goals, you must make sure they are in a direction that is similar to your family goals. Relationships outside of the family can be made that will supplement family goals—your friends should support your family. You must keep yourself in good physical and mental shape so that you are able to reap the harvest that you have spent your life cultivating. You must meet your health goals, or all of your other goals won't matter. And any activity or move you make must be in line with your spiritual goals, or no movement is worthwhile. When all of your goals are congruent, then efforts toward one benefit all.

4. Make commitments

You must become committed to achieving the goals worthy of your efforts. Commitment is a key factor in reaching your goals. Dreaming is easy. Accomplishing a goal takes effort. When you are sure of what you want, you must push forward toward that goal as if you cannot and will not fail.

Johann Wolfgang von Goethe, the German author and philosopher, said, "Until one is committed, there is hesitance, the chance to draw back. Always ineffectiveness. Concerning all acts of initiative (and creation), there is one elemental truth the ignorance of which kills countless ideas and splendid plans; that the moment one commits oneself, then providence moves too. All sorts of things occur to help one that would have never otherwise occurred. A whole stream of events issues from the decision, raising in one's favor all manner of unforeseen incidents and meetings and material assistance which no man could have dreamed would come his way. Whatever you can do or dream you can begin it. Boldness has genius, power, and magic in it. Begin it now."

Persistent commitment is key to reaching your goals. As President Calvin Coolidge said, "Press on. Nothing can take the place of persistence. Talent will not; the world is full of unsuccessful people with talent. Genius will not; unrewarded genius is almost a proverb. Education alone will not; the world is full of educated derelicts. Persistence and dedication alone are omnipotent."

5. List benefits

Imagine what life will be like when you reach your goals. If you explore *why* you want to reach each of your goals, you will create a list of benefits you can expect by accomplishing each goal. Knowing the benefits will help motivate you to get going and keep going in the direction of your dreams. The personal reasons behind the goals will help you do what you have to do.

Sometimes, uncovering the real motivation behind a desire modifies your goal. For example, you might have a goal to obtain a sum of money. If you want the money to pay for medicine or for a surgery, then your real goal is to be healthy. If you want the money to buy entertainment, then your underlying goal is to be happy. If you want money to buy a car, you might ask yourself, "Why do I want a car?" Answer: "To get to work." "Why do I want to get to work?" Answer: "To earn money." "Why do I need to earn money?" Answer: "To buy a car." In this case, it might just be better to stay home. Of course, you would use the car for many other reasons, but sometimes we work for certain goals simply because we think we should.

Within a few miles of my home there are at least seven lakes. One is eight miles long and the deepest in the state, a popular recreation and fishing destination. A client of mine owns a pontoon boat and operates a guide service for wealthy fishermen on that lake. He stays so busy that he often turns anglers away. I asked him why he doesn't buy a few more boats, hire some help, and make a lot more money by managing an expanding business. He asked me why he should set a goal to make more money.

It seemed logical to me: so he could become rich, retire, and do whatever he felt like doing!

He told me that if he retired, he would spend every day fishing, and that is what he was doing right now.

Knowing the benefits of a goal is essential when you have to delay gratification for your efforts, as in getting a college education. When I think about veterinary school, I have very few fond memories of attending classes, completing tedious and mundane laboratory assignments, and studying throughout many nights. I did find the whole experience rewarding, but there

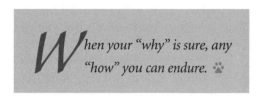

When your "why" is sure, any "how" you can endure. 🐾

were a multitude of things I would rather have done during that period of my life. However, I knew that if I wanted to practice veterinary medicine, I had to make it successfully through college. The benefits of a diploma outweighed the drudgery of the university.

6. Prioritize goals

Consider rewriting your goals in order of priority when the list becomes overwhelming. Ranking the goals can be an efficient way to assure that important things get done before things that seem urgent but are really not as important. Balance the time you spend on each goal according to its priority.

If two goals are diametrically opposed, eliminate one so that you can work toward the more important one. If you are uncertain as to which is more important, postpone both until the answer is clear.

7. Uncover necessary knowledge

When you have prioritized each goal, you should make a list of all the things you will need to do to accomplish each goal. Whatever you establish as a goal, there will always be more you can learn about it. Your resources for information are endless. You might talk with experienced people and learn what they did to accomplish their goals. Realize that many people who have reached their goals would never have done so if they

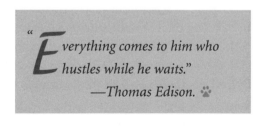

"Everything comes to him who hustles while he waits."
—*Thomas Edison.* 🐾

had known in the beginning what it would cost them in the end. Perhaps your goals will change once you discover what you must do to reach them.

Before you begin your quest, collect information. Think and gather energy while you make your plans. Even though you are not yet moving toward your goal, work on it as if you were. You can research the library and surf the Internet for more information about methods that will help you attain your goals. You need to use technology to your advantage.

> *Reading and studying can produce knowledge.*
> *Meditation and digestion form judgment.*

8. Take action

"Knowledge is power." This old saying is true only when knowledge induces action. Although knowledge has an advantage over ignorance, knowledge alone is not enough. If power were derived from knowledge alone, libraries would rule the world. When you put knowledge into action, then you have the power to create success. People don't get paid for what they know, but rather for what they do with what they know.

> *"The secret of getting ahead is getting started. The secret of getting started is breaking your complex overwhelming tasks into small manageable tasks, and then starting on the first one."*
> —Mark Twain

If the first step toward your goal looks daunting, skip it (if you can). By starting the project with a less formidable task, you can build momentum that can make the first step easier at a later date.

If everything on the list needs to be done and there is no priority, consider putting each item on a separate piece of paper. Turn all the pieces of paper over on a tabletop and then select one piece of paper. Carry out that task and then take another, focusing on one task at a time.

9. List obstacles and plan strategies to overcome them

When your goals are written and prioritized and you are committed to reaping their benefits, nothing can prevent your success . . . except for obstacles.

Somewhere along the journey through life, everyone runs into unplanned roadblocks and detours; or the steps that you thought would easily lead you to the top of the ladder get cluttered with junk. The key that you thought would open the door to your success doesn't even fit in the lock. Sometimes it seems as though you do everything right—you gather the ingredients, mix them properly, and put them into the oven—only to find that someone has shut off the power. You seem to hit barriers that prevent you from advancing and reaching your goals. Obstacles seem to block your progress like a cement wall at the end of an alley.

The walls you hit on the path of life come in many forms. Accidents occur which make your road rougher. Bosses and coworkers impede your professional progress. Sometimes a spouse or children get in your way and delay your personal goals. Bureaucracies and regulations can hinder your plans. Alcohol and recreational drugs can inhibit your ascent. Slippery characters can swindle you and set you back financially. Often self-doubt and feelings of insecurity manage to block your paths toward success. Obstacles give you reasons to stop working on your goals. They allow you to abandon your dreams. They give you excuses to quit.

> "*Success usually comes to those who are too busy to be looking for it.*"
>
> —*Henry David Thoreau* 🐾

From time to time, I have used all of these excuses to explain my lack of success. You might have used other excuses to justify abandoning your goals. These imaginary walls and roadblocks seem very real when you encounter them. But when you look back at them, they are not the same. Once you have gotten past them, they hardly look like obstacles at all.

We will all encounter obstacles that might keep us from achieving our goals. We will be able to deal with such problems better if we prepare for them before they occur. Just as we carry a spare tire in our cars in case we have a flat, we can carry contingency plans for achieving our goals in case we meet a roadblock along the way.

Dale's wall

When I have a problem that seems insurmountable and unfair, or when I am challenged with what appears to be an obstacle or wall in my path, I think of a young man I knew when I was a kid. His name was Dale Rauber. Dale was a few years older than I was, so when I turned fourteen, he was already driving cars. Dale liked cars. He liked fast cars. He liked to squeal his tires when he went around corners. He could burn rubber better than anyone I knew. Someday I wanted to grow up and drive a car like Dale. I never told him he was a role model of mine. That would not have been cool.

I think about Dale when I have difficulties because Dale never got to experience many of the problems that we call obstacles. He never had credit card debt, never felt the pressure of making a mortgage payment on time, and never filed for bankruptcy. He never had an argument with a spouse, never got a divorce, and never struggled to raise rebellious teenage children. He never had a computer hard drive crash without his files backed up, never had his stock market portfolio shrink, and never faced the challenges involved with placing a parent in a nursing home. Dale never got the chance to face the obstacles that we casually curse daily. He never even had a chance to set and pursue adult goals.

Dale had a real obstacle in his life. He hit a real wall that prevented him from reaching his goals. Dale's advancement was not limited by a glass ceiling. It wasn't his gender or his race that prevented his progression. He didn't hit the type of wall that runners do when they just can't go any faster or farther. His obstacle was real and tangible. It was not an illusion. I have seen the wall that Dale encountered. I have touched it. I have shed tears on it. It is not very tall, but it towers over anything I think of as an obstacle in my life. It makes my challenges seem small and insignificant—my problems are but petty pebbles along my path.

No, Dale's wall was not a wall into which he crashed his car after getting drunk one night. It was not a wall from which he fell and broke his neck. It was not the wall of a prison that confined his activities. It was truly a wall one must see firsthand to appreciate its awesome, stirring power.

Dale's black granite wall is massive. It is almost five hundred feet long and supported by 140 concrete pilings driven down thirty-five feet to bedrock. How do I know it is Dale's wall? His name is grit-blasted on it in half-inch letters, line 72, panel 32W, along with over 58,000 other names. It's a hell of a wall. The wall was built with private donations as a lasting tribute to those who served and died with courage, sacrifice, and devotion to duty and country. It is located in a solemn stretch of grass between the Lincoln Memorial and Washington Monument in Washington, D.C. It is 12,000 miles from the jungles of Vietnam where Dale died when he was twenty years, eleven months, and one day.

Although the Vietnam War Memorial is in the mall in your nation's capitol, the image of Dale's wall is right with me whenever I think I have hit an obstacle in my life. Dale's wall reminds me of how trivial my problems are and how fortunate I am to have the opportunity and freedom to experience them. No, I don't think you need to go looking for trouble. But problems should not prevent you from reaching your goals.

> *Just as the silent stream becomes a beautiful babbling brook*
> *when boulders are placed in its path, real obstacles*
> *can make us stronger, better people.*

Perhaps there have been people in your life who encountered obstacles similar to Dale's. Perhaps you know people who have had serious accidents, or diseases, or perhaps you can relate to the students at Columbine or the victims of 9/11. If you are ever in a position that seems hopeless and unfair, think about Dale's wall and the real obstacles that some people face. Realize that there are thousands who would gladly trade places with you. Although your obstacle may appear real, it is something you have the chance to get over, around, or through. When you do, you will realize it was just an *obstacle illusion.*

Another obstacle we will encounter is time. Time is the one thing used more than any other as an excuse for inaction. If you have never used lack of time as an excuse, you are in a very small minority.

"Sorry I didn't call you, Mom. I just didn't have time."
"Sorry I didn't visit you, Grampa. I ran out of time."
"Sorry I can't help you, Sis. I just don't have time."
"I didn't have time to finish the report."
"Maybe I'll have time when the kids are grown."
"Maybe I'll have time after I retire."
"I don't have time to exercise."
"I don't have time to eat balanced meals."
"I don't even have time to return an e-mail."
"If I just had a little more time."

> *We all have time. The difference is what we do with it. Creating your*
> *own life is a full-time job. Stop wasting time trying to change others.*

> "*A*cceptance of what has happened is the first step to overcoming the consequences of any misfortune."
>
> —William James ❖

Without a doubt things happen that really do block your advancement toward your goals. However, many of the obstacles you encounter are self-imposed. Make sure that anything that stands in your way is real, not just something you think prevents your advancement

Accept the fact that there will be obstacles in your path that will appear real and make plans ahead of time to deal with them. Try to anticipate future challenges and decide in advance how you are going to overcome them. Be ready to cope with troubles and move on.

10. Review goals and success often

You need to rethink your goals often. What was important yesterday may not be meaningful today. Urgency and priorities change. So do perspectives and perceptions.

If you practice setting goals that are easy to reach, you will gain experience that will eventually enable you to tackle complex long-range goals.

Stop and reward yourself for reaching small goals. Short-term goals accumulate and become the foundations of larger dreams. You can be creative with your rewards and not limit yourself just to food and money. Bob Nelson wrote a handy book, *1001 Ways to Reward Employees,* about rewards for employees that can be used as a source for personal rewards, as well.

Another way to reward yourself for your accomplishments is to turn the "To Do List" into a "Done List." When you have checked off everything on your list of goals, don't throw the list away. Rather, save and rename it. When you feel as if you aren't getting anywhere in life, you can take a look at your "Done List" and appreciate all that you have accomplished.

Like baking a cake, goal setting can be simple and easy when you follow a recipe. The points listed here give you a basic outline to follow, but you still need to decide what goals you want to pursue and how you will reach for them. The next chapters will help you decide what you really want and how you can set goals for *SMARTER Success.*

From SMART to SMARTER success

*T*he intelligent way to have a happy and healthy life is to learn a proven technique that will help assure you of success. Nobody wants to be dumb. Nobody wants to do something that is stupid. When it comes to striving for success, the dumb way is to completely ignore goals and hope to haphazardly stumble upon success. The more intelligent way is to learn about setting goals for success.

To recapitulate what has been discussed in this book so far:

You need to explore what success means to you personally.
Your definition of success needs to include health and happiness.
You need to know what makes you happy.
Your thoughts create the world you experience.
You can set goals to control the changes that inevitably occur in your life.
You can practice various techniques to set and reach for goals.

What has been discussed so far applies to setting goals in general. Once you know what you really, really want, you can establish a specific goal. The goal you establish will be one of two kinds. You can set a goal to *have* something or to *be* something. (Perhaps one could argue that goals can be set to *do* something, but ultimately we do things either to *have* or to *be* something.)

> *The kind of goal you desire will determine the system you choose to pursue that goal. Once you establish what you want and fully realize why you want it, the path to follow toward your goal will become clear.*

For years, I thought that all kinds of goals were about the same—goals were just goals. Any goal was just something you worked toward. If you reached your goal you were successful. I listened to scores of speakers who talked about goals and said that you could have everything you wanted if you set appropriate goals. I read all sorts of books about goals and success and believed that all the different goal-setting systems were about the same. I followed the directions of the experts and found that the SMART way to set goals worked very well.

The word SMART is an acronym (or perhaps an acrostic) for a technique that has been described and modified by so many speakers and authors that it is difficult to cite the originator. To the best of my knowledge, I have never heard anyone claim it as a proprietary system or technique, but it does work well. SMART is a word you can use to remember the five characteristics of a goal. If you want to *have* something, create a goal that is:

- Specific
- Measurable
- Acceptable
- Realistic
- Time-limited

Some authors have different words assigned to the letters, such as Attainable or Actionable for "A" and Timely for "T", but they mean about the same thing.

> *An acrostic is a word created by taking a letter (usually the first) from a list or series of words or lines. An acronym is a word formed by the first letter of each word in a series of words that are in a particular order. For example, the noun SCUBA is an acronym that comes from self-contained underwater breathing apparatus.*

If your goal is to *have* something, you are much more likely to get it if you define the goal with this method. The SMART system works best when the goal is to *have* something like a house, a car, jewelry, clothes, or toys. It works very well if you want to collect status symbols. If you want money and the things that money can buy, this is the way to get it. I have used it successfully myself many times.

The SMART technique offers a guide to use in establishing a well-described goal. It suggests you set a goal that is:

Specific

You need to identify exactly what it is you want to have. If you want a car, you should describe exactly what kind of car you fancy. Write down the make and model, the color and options that you desire. If you want a house, you can collect pictures or drawings of the house of your dreams, note the size and number of rooms, the landscaping, the type of siding, and the design of the windows. If you are after money, you can declare a specific amount you want to accumulate.

Measurable

If you can't afford your goal right now, you can accomplish your goals in measurable steps. You can make monthly payments on the car. Decide how much you can afford for mortgage payments on a house. Calculate what you will be able to save or invest every month or every week. If your goal can be measured, you can handle small pieces more easily than the whole project at once. By breaking the goal up into pieces or "chunking" the goal, you will be able to celebrate accomplishments and progress along the way.

> "*Start by doing what is necessary, then what's possible, and suddenly you are doing the impossible.*"
> —*St. Francis of Assisi* 🐾

Sometimes you need to take a giant step in the right direction. Sometimes a leap of faith is needed, especially to get things going. However, most projects can be accomplished by taking baby steps that do not appear to be difficult or overwhelming. When a goal that appears intimidating is broken down into measurable steps, little actions can produce big results.

Acceptable

The goal you set must be in line with your personal morals and ethics. Your dream must be within the limits of the laws of society. You are more apt to reach your goal if you have friends and family supporting your progress. If your plans are acceptable to those around you, they may be able to offer you encouragement if you ever get discouraged.

If the goal you set is to own a rusted-out station wagon, you had better check with the community authorities to see if there are laws about having such a car parked on the streets in your neighborhood. Building ordinances and zoning laws may prevent you from building your dream home on the lot you desire. Everything you want to acquire is currently owned or controlled by someone else. However you obtain what you desire, you must make certain it is legal, moral, and acceptable to those who will be parting with their money or property.

Realistic

Your goals should not be outlandish or totally impossible. Growing fields of artichokes in Alaska or raising flocks of sheep in downtown Detroit is not realistic. The car you plan to buy should be within your budget. The house should be within your means, not only to purchase but also to maintain. The income you desire to create must be within reason. Your goal should make you stretch, but not to the point where you snap. It may look impossible to others but that shouldn't stop you if you are certain that your goal is realistic.

Time-limited

Time is of the essence when it comes to SMART goals. Deadlines give life to goals. "Things may come to those who wait," according to Abraham Lincoln, "but only the things left by those who hustle." A deadline forces you to take action and get going on the pursuit of your dreams. Procrastination is your enemy. Time pressure adds urgency and motivates completion.

You should set a date for the purchase of the car and make plans to drive it home. You should set a date for moving into your new home. It may take fifteen, twenty, or thirty years to pay for your house, but it will get paid off in a set amount of time if the payments are made according to the amortization schedule. Set a date to celebrate your new net worth.

The SMART technique works fine if your goal is to have money or things that money can buy. Let's say you want to accumulate $12,000 in savings. That is a specific goal. To do that you could put $500 in the bank each month. That would be a measurable step to take on a regular basis. If you plan to earn the money by working at a legitimate job, your goal will probably not affect other people and would therefore be acceptable. Is it realistic to put $500 away monthly? If you make $6,000 a month, it might be easy. If you make $200 per week, you will need to reset your goal to be more in line with your income. Saving $500 per month for twenty-four months will mushroom into $12,000 plus interest and you will have accomplished your goal in two years, making it time-limited.

If your goal is to have a million dollars, you can adjust the factors involved. Your first step might be to get a better job or more education. Buying lottery tickets might be a way to reach your goal, but statistically it is not very realistic. You can increase your worth by increasing your unique services to others. It might take longer than two years, but a time limit could still be set.

Many people have used the SMART system to become independently wealthy. You can use it to get almost anything you want. You can have enough substance flowing into your life so that you would not have to work another day. You could be so rich that it would be obscene for you to spend all of your wealth. When someone asks how much money you have, you could shrug your shoulders and say, "I dunno." Even your accountant wouldn't know what you are really worth.

How much will you need to have to be really rich? When will you know you have enough? When will you have purchased everything you want?

Money can buy almost any "thing" you want to have

Once you use the SMART technique to accumulate money, you can buy whatever you like. You can use the SMART system to get any *thing* your heart desires. The important key word here is "thing." The SMART technique does work well if your goals are to acquire things. But if you think about what you really want, you will remember that people generally want to have things so they can feel successful and be happy.

If you want to have money, chances are you really don't want it just to collect coins or paper or a portfolio. You probably want to buy something with money, or save it for a sense of security, or purchase something in the future. Chances are that you buy things to make yourself happy. If that is true, then the real reason you want money is to be happy. Happiness is the reason you want to buy stuff. Happiness is your purpose. To be happy is your real goal.

If your goal is to have a spouse, to have children, to have a house or car or toy, chances are you want these things so you can live happily. You want things, but your underlying desire is to have those things so you can be happy.

> **CAUTION!** *Multitudes of people have been disappointed when they tried to find happiness by striving for things they wanted to **have**. Criminals set goals to have things. Thieves want to have money. Addicts want to have drugs. Murderers want to have ultimate power over other people. Warriors fight to have treasures, natural resources, and territory. Dictators struggle to have control and power over more people. All of these individuals are taking something from someone else and seldom getting what they really want in return. If their goals were to **be** rather than to **have**, they would give rather than take.*

The SMART system will definitely help you accumulate material wealth so that you will appear successful, but it might not help you feel successful. If collecting things has not fulfilled your life, perhaps you need to take a closer look at your past goals and those for which you are still striving. If "having it all" still leaves you in need, stop and realize that the real measure of your wealth is not how much you have—rather, it is what you would be worth if you lost everything you own.

> "*No man can tell whether he is rich or poor by turning to his ledger. It is the heart that makes a man rich. He is rich or poor according to what he is, not according to what he has.*"
>
> —*Henry Ward Beecher* ❖

I have used the SMART system and it has worked very well. With this technique I have obtained most everything I ever wanted, including a car, a college diploma, a veterinary practice, a home, and even a family. Yet the SMART system did not help me get me what I ultimately desired.

You can't buy happiness with any amount of money

Over the past decades, I have observed my patients and other animals and noticed how happy and content they seemed to be, most of the time. The animals owned nothing! No clothes. No houses. No cars. No jewelry. No boats. No recreational vehicles. No bank accounts. No stock portfolios. No nothing. They never bought anything. They never went shopping. Yet they seemed to be happy.

When I observed my clients and other humans, I noted that many of them were not happy. People griped about the weather, their families, their schools and jobs. They complained because they didn't have enough money, enough time, or enough of what other people had. Those folks lived in nice, secure homes, worked for decent employers, and seldom missed any meals. Most owned televisions, cars, or trucks, and a whole lot of stuff. They owned so much, yet continually pursued the one thing they lacked and animals naturally possessed.

> "*To be wealthy, a rich nature is the first requisite and money but the second. To be of a quick and healthy blood, to share in all honorable curiosities, to be rich in admiration and free from envy, to rejoice greatly in the good of others, to love with such generosity of heart that your love is still a dear possession in absence or unkindness—these are the gifts of fortune which money cannot buy, and without which money can buy nothing.*"
> —*Robert Louis Stevenson*

Physical possessions can influence our happiness, but only if we choose to *be* happy. I believe most people want to be happy, but they are using the wrong goals to attain success.

The SMART technique does not work very well if your goal is to *be* something. Specific, Measurable, Acceptable, Realistic, and Time-limited are hard to relate to "being" goals. If your goal is to be happy, to be healthy, to be a spouse, to be a parent, to be a friend, or just to be friendly, what specifically does that mean? How can you actually measure happiness or anything else you want to be? Although these goals are acceptable and realistic, they should go on forever and not be limited by time.

When you stop to think about it, happiness seldom comes from having things. You can't *have* happiness; you must simply *be* happy.

> *The simplest of animals know that life is not about collecting things. "To be something" is what really counts. "Being" is what life is all about.*

If you want to *be* something, there is a SMARTER way to establish your goals. This is a system I have developed to maintain health and happiness and create a lifetime of success. The characteristics of this new system are a better fit for goals that guide you in striving to *be* something.

Each of the seven letters in the word SMARTER stands for a characteristic of "being" goals and each will be discussed in the following chapters. SMARTER goals are:

- **S**imple
- **M**eaningful
- **A**ltruistic
- **R**easonably balanced
- **T**imeless
- **E**motionally stabilizing
- **R**elationship building

This novel method of setting goals has been researched, developed, and tested over a ten-year period and will undoubtedly continue to evolve. Although it is original, it is based on ancient and time-tested ideas.

You may not remember what the letters stand for, but if you understand the difference between "*having*" goals and "*being*" goals, you will never forget what the word SMARTER means. The essence of the SMARTER system is straightforward. Rather than

…joining the race to *have* more, set and strive for goals to *be* more.

…pouting because you do not *have* a good friend, try to *be* a good friend.

…jostling to *have* a better job, set a goal to *be* a better employee.

…desiring to *have* a fabulous mate, *be* a desirable mate.

…pleading to *have* kids who respect you, *be* a respectable parent.

…dieting to *have* a perfect body, eat to *be* a healthier person.

…collecting things so you can *have* more status, help others and *be* of more service.

…wanting to *have* a better city, *be* a better citizen.

…wanting to *have* a better neighborhood, *be* a better neighbor.

…fighting to *have* rights, live to *be* righteous.

…struggling to *have* the power of a king, *be* kind to all creatures and the kingdom will be yours.

…working to have more money, work to create more meaning in your life.

…just increasing your net worth, increase your net worthiness.

The differences between setting goals to *have* something with the SMART technique and setting goals to *be* something with the SMARTER system are substantial. If you glean only one idea from reading this book, let it be this:

> *Understanding the difference between setting a goal to be something and setting a goal to have something can determine your health and happiness, and ultimately your success.*

The following list compares and contrasts the qualities of the two systems and will help you understand their advantages and benefits.

		SMART goals	**SMARTER goals**
1.	Type	To *have* something	To *be* something
2.	Control	Others	Self
3.	Substance	Tangible	Intangible
4.	Key idea	Destination	Direction
5.	Shape	Linear	Cyclical
6.	Assessment	External	Internal
7.	Gratification	Delayed	Instant
8.	Failure	Destination missed/abandoned	Progress quit
9.	Character	Vain, egotistic, self-complacent	Humble, tolerant, kind

1. Type of goal

If you want to *have* something, you can use the SMART technique and make the goal specific, measurable, acceptable, realistic, and time-limited. If you want to *be* something, you should use the SMARTER technique and make your goal simple, meaningful, altruistic, reasonably balanced, timeless, emotionally stabilizing, and relationship building.

2. Control

SMART goals that are set to have things depend upon others and factors that can be difficult to control. Everything you want to have—a car, a house, more money—is currently owned or controlled by someone else. Also, once you acquire the thing that you want to have, other people can take it away from you.

SMARTER goals depend upon your own way of thinking. You don't need to take or have anything to be what you want to be. You don't need to have a child to be a parent, because you can adopt an orphan or borrow a niece, nephew, or neighbor and be a parent by doing the things parents do. You don't need to have a friend to be a friend, just do nice things for people. Your health is more dependent upon your own thinking than it is on what disease or condition you have. Your success and happiness are dependent upon your own thoughts. Only your own desires and imagination limit what you can be. No one can take that from you.

3. Substance

SMART goals are tangible. You can see, feel, smell, hear, touch, or taste the results of your efforts. These are things that you can purchase, or they can be given to you. They can be lost or stolen. They can rust, rot, or break.

You can drive the car of your dreams. You can kick the tires, change the oil, and polish the chrome. You can see the house you imagine. You can paint it and mow the lawn and wash the windows. An assessor will help you determine its value so you can pay taxes on it. Neighbors and friends can admire it. The real money you acquire can be stored in a wallet, purse, or vault.

SMARTER goals are different in that they are intangible. You can't actually touch them or see them. They can't be purchased or given to you. They can't be lost or stolen, but they can be forgotten. They are found in the same place where you always can find happiness, kindness, love, peace, and other price-less treasures. They exist only in your mind.

4. Key Idea

The SMART system uses a goal to determine a destination. The goal is reached by getting from where you are now to where you want to be in the future. The journey is a means to an end.

The SMARTER system uses a goal to determine a direction. The goal may never be reached; but rather, it is reached for. The journey doesn't lead you to an end; it guides you along the right path. The goal is the process rather than the product of your life.

5. Shape

SMART goals are linear. They proceed along a flat time line. There is a beginning, which is the time when you establish what you want to have. There is a time when you work on your goal. And there is an end point. If you are successful, the end is a time when the goal is completed, accomplished, or obtained. The end might also be when you miss or abandon the goal.

SMARTER goals are cyclical or elliptical rather than linear. Just as with the SMART system, there is a beginning. It starts with establishing a goal to *be* something. The beginning is the only point in time that has any importance. Once you begin to strive for a SMARTER goal, you are constantly moving toward that goal. The goal is never attained, as there is always room for improvement. "Being" goals are continuously developing. Like the human imagination, "being" goals have no limit or end point. There is no time at which you can say, "There! I've done it!" SMARTER goals go on and on.

If your goal is to be happy or healthy, it is easy to see that you will have to strive continuously toward that goal. Happiness and health are not things you can hold on to. But it seems as though some "being" goals should have end points. If you desired to be a spouse, wouldn't a wedding fulfill that desire? If you wanted to be a parent, wouldn't the goal be accomplished when your child was born? If you wanted to be president of a club, a company, or a country, wouldn't winning the election fulfill that dream? If you wanted to be a doctor, wouldn't graduation mean you had met your goal?

Not quite! Whether your goal is to be a spouse, a parent, a president, or a doctor, getting to the point where you earn a label or title is just the start. Marriage is the beginning of being a spouse. It doesn't end until the partners quit or are separated by death. Birthing a child is just the beginning of being

> "*Your attitude about who you are and what you have is a very little thing that makes a very big difference.*"
> —*Theodore Roosevelt* ❖

a parent, unless you quit or someone dies. An election is the beginning of being a president until you quit or are forced out of office. A diploma from a university allows a doctor to obtain a license and start practicing. The goal to have a college degree has been met, but the goal to be a doctor has just begun. The only way a SMARTER goal stops being a goal is if you quit trying.

6. Assessment

It is much easier to measure things than thoughts. Things are objective and thoughts are subjective. What you *have* can be made obvious to all. What you *are* is not always obvious, even to yourself.

The SMART system allows others to assess your success. Because success is dependent upon what you have, your success can be judged by outside observers. Success is external.

The SMARTER system requires you to assess your own success. Because success is dependent upon what you are, your success can only be assessed by you. Success is internal. It exists in your mind and in your thoughts.

"Success is not so much what you have as it is what you are." Those are the words of Jim Rohn, who has been called America's foremost business philosopher and a master of success. His books and seminars reveal him to be an expert on the subject and a very credible source for information on personal development. He has earned more money than any one person could spend; yet he professes that money and the things money can buy are nothing compared to what you can be.

7. Gratification

In the SMART system, the reward comes when the goal is reached and you have what you originally sought. Gratification can be immense and satisfaction intense, but it is delayed until you earn or obtain what you want. Certainly you can celebrate successful small steps along the way but you are not really successful until you reach your final goal. Reaching your goal is essential to the SMART technique. You must attain your goals so that you receive a physical reward. This will reinforce your desire to set and reach for new goals.

In the SMARTER system of goal setting, the reward comes not when you reach the goal, but when you reach *for* the goal. When you set a goal to be something, gratification comes the minute you realize that you are on the correct course to becoming the person you want to

S MARTER goals are exemplified by the gardener who toils not just for a harvest in the fall but for the pure enjoyment of nurturing the plants throughout the growing season. ❧

be. Although being goals have no end point, they have points along the way where you can stop and assess progress, taking pride in what you have accomplished. You feel successful because you know you are on the proper path; you are taking the right road.

8. Failure

Failure is a risk when setting goals with the SMART technique. If you are not successful in reaching a SMART goal, your attempt is considered to be a failure. Failure can be seen as the opposite of success in this system. If your

attempts at reaching your goal continue to falter, you might see yourself as a failure in general. When self-image and self-esteem take a dive, motivation declines, often to the point where there is little to support the will to live. Psychologists tell us that failure to

P eople might fail many times, but they aren't failures until they give up. ❧

reach self-imposed deadlines and goals is a major source of depression. The feeling of failure might be a significant reason that the suicide rate is so high.

Failure is not a risk with the SMARTER system because you can't fail, unless you just quit. If you are always striving to be something, your efforts continue until you stop trying. And that is a choice you never need to make.

Being goals can prevent frustration with momentary setbacks because there is no hurry. Whatever you are doing, your actions are moving you toward the goal. Sitting still, resting, or enjoying peace are all parts of the process.

9. Character

It has been observed that people who are continually reaching for things or for power tend to become vain and materialistic. They are often conceited and believe they are better than other people who own fewer things or control less power. They demand better service in restaurants, better seats in theaters and airplanes, and better treatment from everyone around them.

On the other hand, people who are always trying to be better people tend to be humble, tolerant, and kind. They are more concerned with serving than with service. They are go-givers rather than go-getters. They tend to live simpler lives that are balanced and meaningful. They have friends who share similar interests and understand success in the same way.

> *When you break from traditional thoughts of success,*
> *when you no longer measure success by what you have*
> *or control, money and power become less important,*
> *and yet, almost like magic, they become more abundant.*

The SMARTER way to think about success involves understanding your own definition of success and happiness, controlling your future by controlling your thoughts, and by setting goals that are simple, meaningful, altruistic, reasonably balanced, timeless, emotionally stabilizing, and relationship building. The next seven chapters will help you understand why and how these elements create *SMARTER Success*.

Simple

Somewhere along the way, we need to realize that *SMARTER Success* can be achieved by setting goals that are simple.

Human beings are the most complex of creatures. Our sophistication leads us to believe we have complex needs. To feel successful, we reach for goals and collect things that demonstrate our success. The desire to prove our success to the world clouds our thinking and we often get confused as to what we *want* and what we actually *need*. Although we are complex creatures, we really don't have complex *needs*. What we *want* may be complex, but what we *need* is elementary. The necessities of life are simple and available to all, while our imaginary desires are boundless and insatiable.

The things we *need* are required for survival. The things we *want* are desired for enriching our lives. Because of advertising, peer pressure, and an escalating standard of living, it is easy to confuse *needs* with *wants*. We may believe we cannot live without the things we want, but to function as successful humans we only need a few simple things.

With few exceptions beyond securing food and shelter, the most important things in life are not physical objects at all. They are concepts, beliefs, convictions, images, thoughts, and characteristics of integrity, respect, and love.

Sometimes we work so hard to get *things* that we don't take time just to *be*. We get so focused on attaining success or obtaining things that we lose sight

🐾 "Showing up is 80 percent of life."

—Woody Allen

of precious, priceless possessions. We don't fully appreciate our families, our friends, our freedoms, our homes, our accomplishments, or the simple, natural splendor that surrounds us.

Sometimes we see only the road ahead of us. We advance along our journey through life like a horse wearing blinders. Although we don't wear harnesses as horses do, it is easy to find ourselves tethered to tasks as though we were no different from beasts of burden. We have jobs to do and we ignore everything else that is going on around us until our chores are finished. We just plod along, unsure of where we are going, assuming we are going in the right direction. It seems as though something or somebody always keeps us moving, just like the driver behind the horse who cracks the whip to keep the cart moving forward.

Blinders, a.k.a. blinkers, really don't prevent a horse from seeing. They are a part of the leather harness a horse wears that enables it to pull a wagon. The straps on the horse's head fasten together to make a bridle. The bridle holds a metal bit in the horse's mouth and also supports the blinders that stick out along the side of the horse's face. These patches of leather prevent the horse from seeing what is behind or alongside of it, forcing the horse to focus on the path ahead without distractions.

If you ever sense that you are just putting one foot in front of the other, plodding down the path of life, or that you are pursuing goals set by other people, stop. Simply stop...and realize that you can escape from your imaginary harness much more easily than a horse can break free from its leather trappings. Shed your blinders and take a look around. As a human being, you don't have to pursue goals the way horses do for their owners. There is no bit in your mouth controlling your speed or direction. You have the freedom to look around

> *"I was raised to sense what someone wanted me to be and to be that kind of person. It took me a long time not to judge myself through someone else's eyes."*
> —*Sally Field* ❧

❧ "Realize that life is an end in itself. Functioning is all there is."
—Oliver Wendell Holmes, Jr.

yourself 360 degrees and make sure you are on the right road headed toward your choice of destinations.

Make certain the path you are on is the one you have chosen by yourself for yourself. Observe and appreciate all the simple scenery along the way as you travel through life. Look at your family and be grateful for the love you share. Cherish your friendships and let your friends know what they mean to you. Treasure your freedoms while you utilize and defend them. Appreciate your home and maintain it with pride. Count your blessings, acknowledge your accomplishments, and observe what you have going for yourself.

The simplicity of animal success

All animals other than humans know instinctively that the ultimate goal of life is to enjoy living. To live today, in the moment, is the only way animals know how to live. They continually "seize the moment." They live day by day. Difficult or easy, living life moment by moment is one of the things we can learn from less complex animals.

By observing success in animals, we can learn that success is simple, but not always easy. Many animals spend most of their resources maintaining and propagating their species. They work hard to find food and shelter just

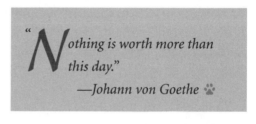

"*Nothing is worth more than this day.*"
—*Johann von Goethe* 🐾

to survive. Granted, some seem to have easier lives than do others. The turtle can stop for the night almost anywhere along its journey because it lives in a natural recreational vehicle; and the hermit crab is the ultimate mooch as it uses someone else's shell as its home. Easy or difficult, successful animal lives are relatively simple.

Animals are successful when they are being what they were meant to be. Even though our species has become the greatest at gathering, what we have still is not as important as what we are. And what or who we are is very simple.

🐾 "All the great things are simple, and many can be expressed in a single word: freedom; justice; honor; duty; mercy; hope."

—Winston Churchill

A dog is successful if it does what dogs do. A watchdog barks at the presence of an intruder. A retriever brings back a fallen game bird. A bloodhound follows a scent to find a lost person. The sled dog pulls a musher through the snow. The seeing-eye dog guides a blind person down the street. The family dog becomes more than just a pet by simply returning unconditional love.

A cat is a cat and that is that. Cats have functioned as pets since the time of the pharaohs in Egypt and are now outnumbering dogs as America's favorite animal companion. Whether a cat is hunting for mice or sunning itself on the windowsill, it will do what cats do and no one should expect any more from it.

Cows are successful when they do what cows do. The female gives birth to a calf and then makes gallons of milk, either for feeding her baby or serving as a foster mother to the human race. Calves grow and mature to create sources of protein and leather.

And a horse is a horse, of course. Successful horses run and jump in the fields, pull wagons, give rides, and provide companionship. They enjoy doing the things they do even when it appears to be work.

Can a cow be more successful than a horse? Is a dog better than a cat? The answers can be debated but they are subjective at best. Species are as different as are individual people. They all have their own skills, talents, and unique characteristics. An ostrich is unable to fly, but it can outrun most birds in flight. A bee can never be an eagle, but it can make honey. A sheep can't run like a deer, but it can produce wool.

To judge which animals are more successful or better than others would be like trying to compare apples with oranges. Animals are all different and therefore incomparable. It is hard to go hunting with a calico cat. It doesn't seem fair to keep a huge St. Bernard in a small apartment, and you wouldn't want one to curl up on your lap. Horses don't play fetch on the lawn very well, and cereal bowls would remain dry if we depended upon dogs for milk.

Whether you are a parent or a child, an employee or an employer, a friend or a spouse, success is not about *having*. It is about *being*. To be successful in life, you simply need to function as you were meant to function. A dog is a dog. A cat is a cat. A cow is a cow. A horse is a horse. And you are a human. You are a human *BEING* —not a human *having*. This simple revelation or clarification of a fact that you already knew will change the way

❧ "Simplicity is the ultimate sophistication."

—Leonardo da Vinci.

you think about success and enable you to understand fully the *SMARTER Success* system.

> *Whenever you hear the words "human being" in the future, they will remind you that success is not about having, it is about being.*

To be or to have

Shakespeare asked the simplest of questions about life, goals, and success: "To be or not to be? That is the question." The six words in this simple question are well known by all of us. Have you ever tried to answer this question? It seems so trivial. To be what? The question seems incomplete. To be alive? To be a person? To be a parent? To be a child? To be a man? To be a woman? To be a spouse? To be a friend? To be rich? To be an employee? To be successful? To be happy? Questions like these are so simple they seldom receive serious thought or answers. Perhaps we are so busy trying to improve what we *have* that we don't take time to improve what we can *be*. Instead of simply working to *be* better, we spend our time working to *have* more.

The importance of *being* goals and *having* goals fluctuates throughout our lives. Typically, each stage of life (juvenile, adult, aged) has a mixture of *being* and *having* goals, but the importance of each type of goal varies. As infants, we have no goals because we believe we own and control everything. Ownership is not an issue for babies. Anything within sight belongs to us. One of the first words we say is, "Mine!" Soon we are told that we must wait until we are older to have what we want. Then we can't wait to advance in age. *Being* goals are very important. We want to *be* five years old to go to school. We want to *be* sixteen or so to get a driver's license. We want to *be* eighteen to vote, or *be* twenty-one for more adult privileges.

> *All too often, we get caught up in waiting for tomorrow and we don't take time just to be what we are today.*

❖ "Fear less, hope more; eat less, chew more; talk less, say more; love more, and all good things will be yours."

—Swedish proverb

As youth we want to *be* something when we grow up. In our childlike imaginations, we can grow up to be anything we dream of being. The possibilities are limitless. Many of us have said, "When I grow up, I want to *be*: a teacher, an astronaut, a firefighter, a doctor, a nurse, an airplane pilot, the President, or anything else. (These aspirations were adequate for older Americans when they were kids, but according to futurist Dan Burrus, the world is changing so quickly that most kids today will eventually have jobs that are not yet invented.)

As we grow older and enter the second stage of life, adulthood, we have more memories of the past upon which to base our expectations for the future. We uncover constraints that seem to limit what we can be and do. We still want to *be* something when we grow up, but the possibilities are circumscribed by negative input from older people telling us what we should do, what we shouldn't do, or what we should not have done. The rules, stated or implied, say we are too old or too young, too tall or too short, the wrong gender or race, or we just don't have enough talent, money, or motivation. The restrictions that limit what we can *be* seem to make no sense and appear neither logical nor fair.

Somewhere along the way, people stop asking us what we want to *be* and start looking at what we *have*. Society measures our worth by what we own and control. Benchmarks of success are things like houses, cars, boats, jewelry, electronics, and other toys. During this period in life, *being* goals are less important, forgotten, ignored, and even shunned. People who are twenty-nine don't want to *be* thirty. People thirty-nine resist *being* forty. We want to *have* youth, vitality, smooth skin, energy, and a whole lot of stuff to make us look successful.

The third stage of life is when our bodies have aged. (It should be noted that this period of life has more to do with biological processes and mental attitudes than chronological ages. We can live vital, independent, and important lives during any stage.) Toward the end of this stage, many of us will enter retirement homes that are filled with elderly people who have sold or given away most of their possessions. Their goals are no longer to *have* things; rather, they talk about *being*. They want to *be* young again. They want to *be* healthy. They want to *be* able to see, hear, and think clearly. They want to *be* free of pain. They want to *be* around their families, but they don't want to *be* a burden to anyone. They want to *be* at peace.

❧ "Creative striving for a goal that is important to *you*...brings happiness as well as success because you will be functioning as you were meant to function."
—Maxwell Maltz, M.D.

> *Even at seemingly mature ages, some people are never able to live in*
> *peace; they have to die before they can really "Rest in Peace."*
> *It is a pity they enjoy such luxury only after they are dead.*

The first and third stages of our lives offer us less opportunity for control than the long middle section. The period between infancy and the infirmary offers us the greatest opportunity to alter our goals and influence our own lives, as well as the lives of others. If we can spend a little more time developing what we want to *be* while we are in the middle of life—the "collecting-stuff-stage"—we can make our golden years happier and healthier and improve childhood for future generations.

At every age there is something we can learn from those who have already experienced what we are going through. Adults tell children, "Be patient. You'll get older soon enough." The elderly advise middle-aged people, "Enjoy life while you still can. It is a shame that youth is wasted on the young." Those who have experienced more of life than we have can give us good advice.

What will you be when you grow up?

When I was thirteen years old, someone asked me, "What do you want to be when you grow up?" I told everyone who would listen that I would be a veterinarian as soon as I could.

Now I realize that I have lived my adult life as a doctor because of the plans of a young kid. I have based my career on the dream of a naïve adolescent. If I were to plan a life for someone else or if I had my life to live over again, I am not sure I would ask a hormone-heavy teenage boy for advice. Even today I am not sure I should continue to plan the rest of my life based on decisions I made previously as a youth. Fortunately, I live in a country that allows me to change my mind and set new goals as I age.

Older individuals, or if you prefer, mature adults, might ask themselves the question asked of children. Instead of asking yourself what you want to be when you grow up, you might ask, "What's in my future? I can't stay at this point in life forever. Has my career reached a plateau? Has my marriage become stagnant? Are my relationships stale? What is the status of my physical and mental health? How will my body change in the years to come? What will I be when I continue to grow up?"

> *"It is never too late to be what you might have been."*
>
> —George Eliot 🐾

Somewhere along the way you might want to step back and take a look at your life to see if you are where you want to be. If you are not, it is never too late to make a change.

What do you want to change in your life? Do you want to lose weight, stop smoking, refrain from biting fingernails, halt arguing with family and friends, curb gambling, stop drinking, stop being pessimistic or negative? These all seem like simple, common goals that anyone might create, but they are all stated in negative terms. Negative goals are hard to attain because they declare where you don't want to be or go. Negative goals establish what you are trying to move away from, stop, or avoid.

> Note: A goal is something you work toward. The reason so many weight-loss diets and smoking cessation programs fail is because they have negative motivations. To lose weight and to stop smoking are negative goals. A health enhancement goal that includes eating healthy food and breathing clean air would be a positive plan to achieve the desired results.

A SMARTER goal should always be stated in a positive way that gives you a direction in which to pursue a desired future. Rather than dieting to lose weight, start eating to be healthy. Rather than trying to stop smoking, set a goal to be healthy by breathing only good quality, smoke-free air. Set positive goals to be friendly instead of grouchy, optimistic instead of pessimistic, positive instead of negative. Instead of criticizing or ridiculing, be a person who praises as often as possible.

Your condition is not so much the situation you are in but your attitude toward it

Near my home in Wisconsin there is an Amish community where I have helped care for animals. Animals are essential to the simple Amish existence. Every farm has a dog and a few cats. Most Amish people raise dairy cattle, pigs, and chickens, and, of course, they all have horses. The horses pull buggies and wagons to provide transportation. The larger horses provide the power to cultivate the fields and haul feed, seed, and the harvest.

Simplicity is one of the standards of the Amish community. Even if a task would be easier with modern technology, they choose to keep things simple and work the old-fashioned way. Compared with other people in our area, the Amish live very simple lives: no electricity from the power company— therefore no light bulbs, no refrigerator, no television, no radio, no vacuum cleaner, no water heater, no microwave. There is very little plumbing in their homes—most utilize an outhouse. Their clothing is white, black, or blue without prints or variety. They work from sunup to sundown.

The Amish women work the gardens by hand. They make their own clothes. They pickle and preserve their own vegetables, pork, and beef. They make their own bread from scratch. They push a rotary lawn mower by hand. They raise chickens and gather eggs.

The Amish children help with the chores, walk or drive buggies to school, and return home to help with more chores. Once they reach the eighth grade, they are finished with school and begin working to support the family.

The Amish men drive teams of horses to plow the fields, plant the crops, and gather the harvest. They toss the feed sacks about by hand. The hay is put up by hand and fed by hand. The animal pens are bedded by hand. The cows are milked by hand into buckets that are poured into milk cans that are cooled by well water in the milk house. The stalls are cleaned with pitchforks and shovels. The soiled bedding is spread in the fields with a horse-drawn manure spreader.

At one time I envied the Amish lifestyle. They don't suffer the stress of the traffic jams found in cities. No waiting lines at gas stations. No flat tires. Computers do not accelerate their lives. Technology neither complicates nor simplifies their way of living. They don't pay electric bills. I thought that living a simple life could ensure success.

Over the years I became a friend of an elder in the community, Clarence. He is one of the leaders of the community and is regarded as a successful farmer. I asked him what it was like to live such a stress-free life. I thought it must be nice not to have to worry about things the way the rest of the world does. I wondered if people in his community ever got stomach ulcers due to stress.

Clarence surprised me with his answer. He said that he himself had an ulcer. He reminded me that he had a dozen children. They had caused his hair to turn gray. One child left their community and religion to join the mainstream culture. One daughter married a boy from outside of their religion and moved far away. One child died of leukemia. His best horse foundered. One of his cows had a twisted stomach. His crops were affected by drought just like everyone else's. His Amish life was different, but he still experienced stress.

If we measure success with money and the things money can buy, and then compare the Amish to average Americans, the Amish might be viewed as unsuccessful. They own very few things and live in poverty by many standards. However, if we allow them to measure their own success, we might end up with a very different conclusion. Most of the people I know in the Amish community appear to be very happy and healthy. They do not look at success the way typical capitalists do.

Just as wealth does not guarantee happiness, simplicity alone does not assure success. Those who live a simple life are not better or happier or more successful than anyone else. On the other hand, they do not appear to be any less happy or at peace than the people who live in mansions or big cities. Prosperity is relative and is best evaluated by the individual in the situation. Like everyone else, they can be successful in their own way by meeting basic needs, striving to be the kind of people their religion dictates, and choosing to believe they are successful in how they live.

The Amish community clearly demonstrates that our success is determined not by the situation we are in but rather our attitude toward it.

A simple goal: to be content

To be content with what you have in a world that is constantly trying to sell you more can be challenging. Can you ever accumulate enough material wealth to be content? It depends upon your point of view.

Maybe you are already independently wealthy and don't realize it. Dale Carnegie wrote, "If only the people who worry about their liabilities would think about the riches they do possess, they would stop worrying. Would you sell both your eyes for a million dollars... or your legs... or your hands... or your hearing? Add up what you do have, and you'll find that you won't sell them for all the gold in the world."

What do you need to have to be content?

Alexander the Great had a simple goal: conquer the world. But even if he had become "king of the world," he would not have been content. His desire for power would not have been satisfied with world domination. The epitaph of Alexander the Great reads, "A tomb now suffices him for whom the whole world was not sufficient."

You will never be content with what you have until you are content with what you are. People all over the world have repeated this idea in adages handed down over the centuries.

- A Japanese proverb translates to, "He is poor who does not feel content."
- An old German belief is, "Contentment is worth more than riches."
- An old English saying states, "A wise man will desire no more than what he may get justly, use soberly, distribute cheerfully, and leave contentedly."
- The greatest wealth is contentment with little.
- To be content with little may be difficult, but to be content with much is impossible.
- And a new American platitude offers, "When you find satisfaction knowing that you are on the right path to be something worthy, you will be content with whatever you have."

It is a simple goal to be more appreciative of all that is around you. It costs no money and takes little effort. Wherever you are in life, the appreciation of all that surrounds you is far more valuable than any control you might claim over it.

A simple goal: to be healthy

Your body is constantly changing. You are always making new red blood cells and filtering out old. Hair grows and falls out. Your skin cells and digestive system cells die, slough off, and are replaced. When you consider that you are constantly changing—building new body parts every day—you realize how important it is to consume the right foods, water, and air. You must be aware of what you are doing to fuel your body and promote healthy functions within it.

People in America spend very little time and money trying to stay healthy compared to how much they spend trying to stop disease and illness. Good health is something people seldom appreciate until they no longer have it. We seldom think about our health until we feel ill or become sick. Then we look for something to cure the disease.

The way you think about your health and how you perceive the challenges of disease can make a world of difference in how you live your life. Do you think about staying healthy every day or do you wait until you are sick and then try to regain health? Do you believe the adage, "No pain, no gain?" Do you wait for pain to set in, or do you do things to avoid pain? Do you believe that there are powerful germs out in the world that are just waiting for the chance to attack your body? Do you believe cancers are stronger than your immune system? Do you feel your body's natural defenses are able to keep you healthy even if challenged by disease?

If health is important to you, try looking at disease from this simple perspective. Imagine entering a dark, unlit room. The room is so dark that you can't see the walls or your hand in front of your face. You can't even see where you are walking so you shuffle your feet, hitting things with your toes before you move forward. You hold your hands out in front of you and wave them wildly trying to feel obstacles in your path. You bump into furniture, knock things off tables, bumble and stumble and make quite a mess.

What could you do to see in the room better? What could you do to help you see where you are going? The darkness that fills the room presents a serious situation. If you could just get rid of the darkness you could see, walk, and move without any trouble. The darkness is the problem, but how do you get rid of it? How do you turn off the darkness? There is no darkness switch on the wall that can be flipped. There is no piece of furniture or equipment that can eliminate the darkness. You could ask for someone to help you turn off the darkness, but there is no one in the world who can do that for you. Nobody can turn off the darkness because it can't be done.

Trying to turn off darkness is a negative approach to increasing visibility. Even a small child knows that you don't try to turn off the darkness—you turn on a light. That is a positive approach.

> *There is not enough darkness in the world to put out the light of one little candle.* 🐾

You can move a switch on a wall, push a button on a lamp, light a candle, open a curtain, squeeze a flashlight, or flick your Bic® (lighter). Nobody tries to turn off darkness. Darkness has no power of its own. You simply turn on the light and the darkness disappears.

Turning on the light to stop the darkness seems so logical; yet when it comes to sickness, we attempt to turn off the darkness by trying to stop the disease. When we get sick, we go to a doctor. The doctor makes a diagnosis and recommends a treatment to stop the illness and pain. The therapy tries to turn off the darkness of disease. Modern medicine can work magic and countless lives have been saved with antibiotics, steroids, hormones, and other drugs. However, most disease can be lessened, eliminated, or prevented not by trying to turn off the darkness but by simply turning on the light.

You can remain healthy by keeping the light shining brightly. To do that, drink the purest water possible. Eat healthy portions of healthful foods. More than 80 percent of all medical problems are directly related to diet. If you are overweight, the best thing you can eat to reestablish your optimal weight is...LESS! Because smoke clouds the light in your lungs, breathe the cleanest air possible. Exercise your muscles, bones, ligaments, and tendons, as well as your brain. Think healthy positive thoughts and cultivate your mind. Changing your thinking can cure psychosomatic diseases. Negative thoughts of blame, hatred, jealousy, and anger are at the root of many diseases. They need to be plucked from our thinking like weeds from a garden.

> "*Ask not that events should happen as you will, but let your will be that events should happen as they do, and you shall have peace.*"
>
> —*Epictetus* ❧

A simple goal: To be at peace

A simple goal that supports health and happiness is to be at peace with yourself and the world. Perhaps peace of mind is the simplest of goals in the area of your spirituality and religion. Peace of mind is found when you accept your beliefs as truth and your actions are in accord with your spiritual thoughts.

Every year in October, my family asks me what I want for my birthday. Birthday presents are a part of our culture and my family always tries to give me something I want. They know that I prefer gifts that cannot be purchased, for example, gifts that are hand-made by the giver, or personalized in some way. My answer to the gift question is usually the same whether it is a birthday, Father's Day, or Christmas. What I want is simple. I tell them that all I want is world peace.

Two words. Is that simple request asking too much? It is a simple request, yet ridiculous. How could anyone deliver such a gift? Mahatma Gandhi, Martin Luther King, Jr., Mother Teresa with the Sisters of Mercy, and Jesus of Nazareth tried to develop peace on earth. They dedicated most of their lives to securing world peace; yet wars are still being waged everyday somewhere on the planet.

The words of Black Elk, a nineteenth-century Native American religious leader, describe the true meaning of peace. "The first peace, which is the most important, is that which comes from within the souls of men when they realize their relationship, their oneness, with the universe and all its powers, and when they realize that at the center of the universe dwells Wakan-Tanka, and that this center is really everywhere, it is within each of us. This is the real peace, and the others are but reflections of this. The second peace is that which is made between two individuals, and the third is that which is made between two nations. But above all you should understand that *there can never be peace between nations until there is first known that true peace which is within the souls of men.*"

> "*When the power of love replaces the love of power, the world will know peace.*"
> —*Jimi Hendrix* ❧

When you first hear someone ask for world peace, you might think the request is impossible. World peace is improbable because nature is naturally turbulent. There will always be conflict, crisis, and fighting somewhere. Struggle is a natural part of our existence. If people aren't fighting with other people, there are critters in the animal kingdom to undo the peace. Whether it is a tiger or a tsetse fly, the animal kingdom provides predators and pests that can produce conflict. People somewhere are always fighting the weather or the climate, a cold, cancer, or the flu. Global peace may never be possible.

But the peace I seek is not in the world out there.

If you think of world peace as being peace within your personal world—the world you experience from day to day and not the far-off reaches of the planet—then there is hope that

L et there be peace on earth, and let it begin with us. ❧

you can realize such peace. Does it matter that there is a war on another continent or fighting in another country if you don't know about it? Does it matter if there is conflict in another city or community? Does it matter if there is unrest in someone else's family or relationship?

Of course, what happens outside your sphere of perception can matter. Other countries, communities, and families, as well as forces of which you are unaware, influence your life all the time. When countries fight, soldiers die and resources are wasted. When communities quarrel, citizens get involved with time and tax dollars. If your parents or your kids aren't getting along, the friction rubs off on you. But everything that happens in other countries, other communities, and other relationships is out of your direct control. You may be able to influence others, but the only world you can really control is the world you create, experience, and perceive for yourself in your own mind. The conflict you are capable of creating or resolving in your mind is comparable to any conflict in the outside world. By creating peace with yourself, you create peace within your own personal world. To do so is a giant step in establishing world peace, at least from an individual perspective.

Even a goal as monumental as world peace can be thought of as simple when you realize that the whole concept of peace begins with a single simple thought. World peace begins with controlling yourself, your own life, your own thoughts. When you

"P eace is not the absence of conflict, but the presence of God no matter what the conflict."
—Anon. ❧

have control over your own peace, you can influence others. If you think that your world is in terrible turmoil, that is your reality. If you are unaware of the fighting going on elsewhere in the world, if the only world you observe is quiet and tranquil, then your world is at peace.

It is doubtful that anyone can ever create global peace. Several have come close, but they were assassinated or crucified by people who were fearful that ideals of peace might spread. The governments and individuals who ended the lives of the enlightened were afraid that world peace might disrupt the anarchy upon which power thrives.

The simplest of goals: to be yourself

To be what you are meant to be is the simplest of personal goals. However, it's not easy to know just what you should be.

In college I had a friend named Jerry Foster. During our sophomore year, Jerry's father died of a heart attack while driving alone in a Christmas snowstorm. Jerry's dad had wanted him to be the first in their family to have a college diploma, so Jerry dedicated his struggle in school to his father's memory. Once Jerry graduated, his father had wanted him to return home and eventually run the company where he'd worked for thirty years.

> "*To be nobody but myself in a world which is doing its best, night and day, to make me the same as everybody else means to fight the hardest battle any human being can fight and never stop fighting.*"
>
> —*e. e. cummings* ❧

Jerry loved to play football and baseball, but he gave up sports in college to follow the career track his father had planned for him. He loved to party, but declined invitations to social events because he thought his dad wanted him to study instead. He worked hard to please his father and to honor his father's wishes.

Upon graduation, Jerry took the job he thought his dad would have wanted him to accept. Then he worked hard for advancement. Somewhere along the way, Jerry did find time to get married. He and his wife had three children. However, they never had time for a vacation. Jerry was always too busy at work to get away. He wanted to coach baseball and soccer, but he often worked fifty and sixty hours a week trying to get ahead. Jerry wanted to spend more time with his wife, but he was always trying to live up to the expectations he believed his father had for him.

Late on the night of December 21, Jerry was driving home from the office. He had a lot on his mind. Production at the plant was down and he was getting pressure from his fellow executives to increase profits. He was worrying about his future at the company and whether or not he was meeting the expectations of the board of directors. He was concerned about his relationship with his wife and if he was meeting her expectations as a spouse. He was worrying about his kids and if they missed having their father for childlike play and meaningful talks. He was worrying about Christmas presents and holiday parties, and year-end bonuses that might not be disbursed. And Jerry wondered if his father approved of what he was doing with his life as he looked down from above.

Then, without warning, Jerry felt a sharp pain in his chest. The fact that his father died of a sudden heart attack about this time of year worried Jerry even more. He pulled off the road, dialed 911, and requested an ambulance ride to the hospital. When the paramedics arrived, they found Jerry slumped over the steering wheel, unconscious. Before he passed out, he had the sense to turn off the engine and turn on the car's emergency flashers. The ambulance crew started CPR and rushed Jerry to the emergency room where over the next few days he slowly recovered.

When I visited him in the hospital, he shared his near-death experience with me. Jerry said he dreamed he went to heaven where he no longer had worldly worries, but he felt apprehensive about reuniting with his father. Jerry had worked hard to live up to his father's expectations, but he only achieved the position of vice president of the company, not president.

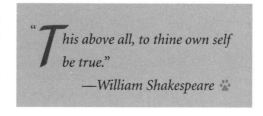

"*This above all, to thine own self be true.*"
—*William Shakespeare*

Jerry went on to tell me that when he eventually met his dad, his father was only mildly disturbed. He said to Jerry, "I am not disappointed you did not become president. I am disappointed that you never became Jerry."

The lesson Jerry shared with me that day has always reminded me of how important it is to follow my own dreams, no matter how much I think others want me to go another way. It also taught me that I must allow people around me to have their own personal goals and to honor their right and freedom to pursue their own dreams. I can set expectations for my family, my employees,

> " *To be what we are, and to become what we are capable of becoming, is the only end in life."*
> —*Robert Louis Stevenson* 🐾

or my friends, but their goals should be their own so that they can become whatever they desire to become.

The greatest success may be experienced by striving for the simplest goal—to be happy and healthy as you watch and participate in the life that unfolds before you.

Those who are truly successful know that SMARTER goals are simple.

Meaningful

Somewhere along the way, we need to realize that *SMARTER Success* can be achieved by setting goals that are meaningful.

We all want to believe our lives make a difference. Hence, we seek to know our purpose. We ponder the age-old questions, "What is the meaning of life? Why do we do what we do? Who cares? Does anyone really appreciate our existence?" While I don't have all the answers, somewhere along the way I have discovered a few ideas that may help you find meaning in your life.

> "*The deepest principle in human nature is the craving to be appreciated.*"
>
> —William James 🐾

Life is like a book

When I was a senior student in the veterinary school at Michigan State University, I was fortunate to meet Dr. Charles Coy. He was an older veterinarian on the teaching staff who had spent many years as a private practitioner for farm animals. He had

---

🐾 "When we are motivated by goals that have deep meaning, by dreams that need completion, by pure love that needs expressing, then we truly live life."

—Greg Anderson

also been in the Peace Corps before joining the faculty at MSU. It was his job to give students hands-on experiences. With Dr. Coy, students practiced taking medical histories, examining live animals, and communicating with real clients. Sometimes we rode along with him to local farms to treat patients when there were emergencies.

During our conversations while traveling to and from the farms, Dr. Coy told us about his Peace Corps adventures. He spent most of his time in Swaziland, Africa, working with cattle. We all thought it was interesting, but we weren't sure we wanted to dedicate two years of our lives to living and working in a country that did not have running water, shopping malls, or televisions. Still, we contemplated the idea of going to a poor developing country to help the residents manage their livestock. If we were to go, we all thought we would need to bring a few veterinary medical reference books. If we were limited to one book, it would be the *Merck Veterinary Manual.*

The *Merck Veterinary Manual* has been the reference book of choice for animal doctors since it was first published in 1955. It is concise and compact, easy to reference, and well written. The 8th edition measures only about eight inches by five inches and is two and a half inches thick. The *Merck Manual* has a fine leather-like cover, and the chapters are easily accessed with scooped finger catches. The print inside the book is small and the pages are thin because of the tremendous amount of information they contain. Anyone can read the book and learn about nutrition, husbandry, and diseases of all sorts of animals. The book contains information on viruses, bacteria, drugs, therapies, normal blood values, gestation periods, body temperatures, and much, much more. It is an incredible book, at least to someone interested in veterinary medicine.

To people who are not interested in animals, the *Merck Veterinary Manual* might be nothing more than a moderately heavy book—a fine leaf-presser. To some people the book is just a book—a sturdy cover wrapped around pages of paper and ink. The thing has no meaning to those who cannot relate to what it contains.

The cover of the book and the printed pages are what everyone can see and use to make judgments about the book. The cardboard, paper, and ink that are bound into the book are like our physical bodies and our material posses-

❧ "The life of the individual only has meaning insofar as it aids in making the life of every living thing nobler and more beautiful."

—Albert Einstein

sions. We can see, feel, and even smell the tangible parts of a book and the things we own. And just as in life, the intangible things—the ideas in the book—are what make the book meaningful and valuable to those who appreciate the information.

> *The ideas within a book are what give it purpose.*

The meaning and purpose of your life come from neither your cover nor your pages. Meaning comes from your content. Meaning is created by what you are continuously becoming.

A goal with meaning gives your life purpose, and your life is most meaningful and worthwhile when your purpose has value. A meaningful goal, one that you truly believe is possible and worthy, can instill in you the will to do almost anything and the motivation to live life to its fullest.

When the why is sufficient, the how will become obvious. You will naturally read and study all you can about what you want to be. You will associate with people who have similar goals. You will seek expert advice and listen to the wisdom of those who have previously aspired to accomplish what you wish to become.

Being goals that have purpose draw out your potentials and assure success. The nineteenth-century British statesman, Benjamin Disraeli, concurred when he said, "The secret of success is constancy of purpose." Purpose differentiates goals from whimsical wishes or fleeting desires. Purpose produces willpower, and where there is a will, there is a way. Willpower is needed to accomplish difficult goals. If you have ever tried to stop smoking, refrain from drinking alcohol, or lose weight, you know that dogged, dedicated willpower is necessary to force yourself to do what you may not want to do, but know that you must.

Animals, instincts, and the meaning of money

Animals have meaningful instincts that may appear to look like goals. They naturally need and desire water, food, shelter, protection, and breeding areas. They must meet those instinctive goals or they will perish. If the fox does not catch the

❖ "Strength does not come from physical capacity. It comes from an indomitable will."
—Mahatma Gandhi

> "*We are not here to merely make a living. We are here to enrich the world, and we impoverish ourselves if we forget this errand.*"
> —Woodrow T. Wilson 🐾

rabbit, it means going hungry. If the salmon does not climb up the rapids, it means dying without propagating the species. If the deer doesn't find forage, it means starvation. If the beaver doesn't build the dam, it means its den will freeze closed in the winter. Animal goals (instincts) are meaningful in that if they are not met, animals perish.

Like animals, humans have similar needs, but our goals go beyond the natural necessities of life. We set goals to have things that are artificial and often unattainable. Money is the most desired goal by those who define success by what they own or control. When our goals for power and money are not met, we don't perish, but we often suffer from depression and anxiety.

A goal to have money has no purpose. Money has no meaning if it is not spent. However, if money is accumulated to support a worthy cause, then it is the worthy cause that makes the money meaningful. The way you spend money is what gives it meaning.

Is your life significant?

Sometimes we get down. And sometimes we have doubts. We wonder why we are here and what life is all about. Why do we go on doing what we do? Who cares? What is it all for? Are we doing any good?

It is easy to think that you are not important. If you look up at the heavens on a dark, clear evening when you are away from tall trees, buildings, and streetlights, you can see as many as six thousand stars. Some of the stars that appear as tiny twinkles of light are really a thousand times bigger than the sun. With telescopes and electromagnetic wave collectors you can "see" even more. Scientists tell us there are some 200 billion billion stars in the universe. That's over 30 billion stars for every human on our planet!!! (The business that charges a fee to name a star after an individual will never run out of stars to register.)

🐾 "The purpose of our lives is to give birth to the best which is within us."
—Marianne Williamson

The size of the universe is beyond comprehension. When you think about the seemingly endless universe, you realize that the earth is rather small. In comparison with the universe, you are like a grain of salt dissolved in all the water of the Atlantic Ocean. Maybe you are even less than that compared with the vast galaxies that surround the Milky Way. You are comparable to a single proton in the nucleus of a chlorine atom mixed in all the oceans of the planet. Relative to the size of the universe, you are extremely small. Relative to the universe, your size is insignificant.

The light from the average star you see at night left that star eighty thousand (80,000) years ago and traveled to reach your eyes at a speed of 186,000 miles per second. That's over 600 million miles per hour. The closest star to earth other than our sun is Proxima centauri. It is 25 trillion miles away, give or take a hundred miles. It takes light over four years to get here from that star. Again, that is the closest star outside of our solar system. The sun is only 93 million miles away, a trip of eight minutes traveling at the speed of light. Relative to time in the universe, your life is extremely short. Relative to the universe your lifetime is insignificant.

There are over six billion people on our planet. When you consider the huge population of the world, it is easy to think you are just one seemingly unimportant individual. Compared to the population of the whole world, your life is insignificant.

Despite your size, the length of your life, and the number of other people on earth, you are still the most significant force within your own world, when you define your world as the environment in which you live and everything you perceive. Without you, the rest of the world does not exist, at least, from your perspective. The world *does* revolve around you, figuratively speaking.

From one perspective you are practically nothing. From another point of view, you are everything. ❖

Since your life is the only one that you can directly control, it is the most important life to you. By living with purpose and making your life meaningful, you can increase your significance and have positive effects on the lives of others.

❖ "So long as you can sweeten another's pain, your life is not in vain."
—Helen Keller

The water bucket test

What difference can one life make in the world? What difference will your life make? Here is a test I learned thirty years ago that you could use to determine whether or not you really make a difference. Try this:

1. Take a gallon bucket and fill it two inches from the top with water.
2. Observe the bucket and water.
3. Stick your hand in the water.
4. Swish your hand around for a few minutes.
5. Pull your hand out.
6. Observe the bucket and water.

This exercise demonstrates how much your life means to the world. At the end of the test, everything looks the same as before your hand went into the bucket. The water represents the world. Your hand represents your life. You enter the world, stir things up, and leave it just as it was before you entered. This analogy of the world and this explanation of life could make you think that you are insignificant. Your life is really trivial and meaningless.

A sociology professor told our class about this test when I was in college. I think he was trying to make students feel less important so they would fit into the system at the university and eventually into the public workforce when they graduated. I think he wanted everyone to conform to the standards established by society.

Many people look at life in this way and believe they really don't matter. We stick our hand in the water and make some waves, but after we pull it out, everything looks the same. What difference can one individual make? The world is so big and there are so many people that one little life can't have much meaning. If we look at life this way, life has no meaning; there is no purpose to life.

All too often we feel unappreciated, useless, and of little value. We feel we have failed if we didn't win the race, become the best, or get all the way to the top. We look at life the way we view the pail of water and assume we make no difference. Things never change and what we do really doesn't matter.

But there is another way to look at this water bucket test that can demonstrate your significance.

🐾 "Ability may get you to the top, but only character and purpose will keep you there."
—Anon.

A veterinarian's view of the water bucket test

When it is not practical to haul cattle, pigs, horses, or sheep to a veterinary clinic, a veterinarian takes everything needed for examinations and treatments to the animals. Working around big farm animals can be dirty work, so most vets wear rubber boots to protect their shoes and coveralls to keep their clothing clean. It is common for hands, attire, and most everything else to become soiled with animal fluids too distasteful to mention. Since sinks and running water are seldom available near animal pens, veterinarians carry a bucket filled with warm water for washing hands, boots, instruments, and patients.

Almost every farm call I make starts with filling a bucket with water for washing hands and boots. The practice began when I was a teenage veterinary assistant with our local veterinarian. It was my job to fetch the bucket of water on each farm. I quickly learned the location of each farmer's faucets, which were usually in the milk house located just off the dairy barn. When I was a college student traveling through Denmark in Europe, I rode with a Danish veterinarian, Poul Hauge, who trained his clients to get the water for him. They even provided soap and a towel. I thought that was a clever idea, but I could never train clients in my area to do that for me.

After every dirty procedure on every farm I have visited over the past thirty-five years I have washed my hands in a bucket of water. I am easily an expert when it comes to putting hands into buckets of water and pulling them out. I have actually taken the water bucket test described above countless times.

While I was a student, I agreed with the college professor and his simple interpretation of the water bucket test. The hand goes in, makes a few ripples, comes out, and everything is the same. But then I began to notice what should have been obvious all along. My hand came out of the bucket wet with water. I had taken something from the pail. The bucket appeared the same but it was different because it had less water in it. My hand was wet but clean. What had previously been on my hand was now in the water. Depending on what I washed off, the water might be tinted brown, red, or the color of some other natural farm by-product that had been on my hand.

Yes, we do enter the world like the hand that dips into the bucket. And yes, we can make quite a commotion while in the water and in the world. And when we leave the water or this world, it will all look pretty much as it did before. But there will be a difference. Our entry into the world changes the lives of parents, grandparents, siblings, neighbors, and future friends and families. We do add a little color to the world or at least tint a portion of it.

History books describe the lives of individuals who have become famous for making significant changes in the world and influencing the lives of many other people. If they conducted the water bucket test the results would seem as though they had food coloring on their hands when they put them in the water. When they took their hands out, everyone could see a major difference in the water. The water would become colorful due to their presence.

Stories of such individuals can make you feel inferior. If you compare yourself to celebrities, political and religious leaders, and other famous people, you may think that their lives had purpose while yours is meaningless. It is unlikely that you could ever accomplish anything close to what they have done. How could your life ever have as much significance as the life of Christopher Columbus, Abraham Lincoln, Mohammed, Buddha, or Jesus of Nazareth?

Perhaps you won't become famous for what you contribute to the world, but it is only your perception that makes you feel inferior, and that point of view can change. Realize that most people who have lived in this world never heard of any of your heroes. The lives of leaders and champions you idolize were meaningless to the people who lived in previous civilizations or might be to those who live now in distant countries. The people you look up to were important to their times and cultures, but they were significant only to those whose lives they touched. You know of them because of your education and heritage. Likewise, people with different backgrounds have their own heroes of history. Fame, prestige, and notoriety are like beauty. They exist only in the eye of the beholder.

We could argue about who has been the most important person in history, but whomever you would support, I would contend that the parents of that individual were equally as significant. Without parents, none of us would exist. Every individual who has had a meaningful life has had help, and it usually started with a parent, the most important person on earth to a child. As people progress through life, they are touched and aided by others. A mentor may develop one pro-

> "*It is not the quantity of things we do in life, but the love with which we do it.*"
>
> —*Mother Teresa* ✢

tégé who will influence the lives of millions of people. A teacher may mold a student into a person who will become a world leader. An employer may help an employee advance to a position of great power and authority. Everyone makes a difference to someone at some time.

> "*And even if you have failed at all else in the eyes of the world, if you have a loving family, you are a success.*"
> —*Og Mandino* ❧

By just *being*, we have meaning. A baby who develops into a good son or daughter makes a meaningful contribution to the world of the parent. The parent who nurtures and provides for a child has great meaning to the child. A spouse who loves and cares for you when you need help adds meaning to your life, and you can reciprocate. Even if only your family thinks of you fondly, you have meaning. In someone's eyes you are a very significant person.

To the people who depend upon you, you may be the greatest man or woman in the world. That makes your life extremely significant and meaningful. And whenever you interact with others, you have the chance to make a difference and create a lasting legacy of your own. It is never too late to reach out to someone and make a difference. It is never too late to create a purpose for your life. Live by the words attributed to William Penn, "If there is any good deed I may do or any kindness I can show, let me do it now for I may not pass this way again."

> "*The influence of each human being on others in this life is a kind of immortality.*"
> —*John Quincy Adams* ❧

Understanding the starfish story

There is an old inspirational story about an elderly man in Maine who walked along the beach with his grandson. The child picked up a starfish from the sand and threw it into the ocean. "If I left it up here on the sand," the boy told his grandfather, "it would dry up and die." He picked up another and repeated the process. "I am saving their lives," he said.

"But," protested the old man, "the beach goes on for miles, and there are hundreds of starfish. What you are doing won't make any difference."

The boy looked at the starfish in his hand and answered, "It makes a difference to this one." Then he gently threw it into the ocean.

The story has been told over and over again. You are led to believe that the actions of the little boy may have seemed trivial, but were meaningful to the starfish that were thrown back into the sea. The tale teaches that a little effort can make a big difference. The story doesn't mention that the tide comes in and out several times a day and that the starfish might have wanted to stay where they were until the tide picked them up again. The tale doesn't relate that many of the starfish were already dead from dehydration and that the boy was simply giving some of the creatures a burial at sea.

> "*Believe that life is worth living and your belief will help create that fact.*"
> —William James

So maybe the boy's actions didn't really matter. Maybe he was upsetting the local ecosystem. But the story points out that the little boy thought he was helping the starfish. That made him happy. It was his intent that made him feel the way he did. To him, his purpose justified his action. He created meaning in what he was doing. The old man thought his action was meaningless while the boy thought it was significant.

> *To be happy is a meaningful goal, especially when you create so much happiness that you have enough to give some of it away.*

What is the meaning of life?

If you think there is no meaning to your life, your task is to create it. Don't expect to find life worth living until you make it that way. You take a giant step toward attaining success when you stop searching for the meaning of life and realize that life has no meaning. Only you have meaning.

You define your purpose by the goals you pursue.

Those who are truly successful know that SMARTER goals are meaningful.

Altruistic

Somewhere along the way, we need to realize that *SMARTER Success* can be achieved by setting goals that are altruistic.

*A*ltruism is the opposite of selfishness and the antithesis of greed. It means concern for the welfare of others. Altruism is *selflessness*.

Perhaps we are all selfish to some extent. When I was sixteen, Mr. Fortin was my driver education instructor. One day we got off the subject of cars and traffic laws and talked about philosophy. He held that whatever we do in life, every action we take, we do for our own personal benefit. Whatever we do, we do for ourselves. People are naturally selfish.

At first I disagreed with Mr. Fortin. I tried to offer circumstances when his doctrine was not true. I asked him, "How about when a parent gives a child food, candy, or clothes? Certainly that is unselfish." He answered that parents do those things because they are expected to do so or because the parents antic-ipate improved behavior, a good deed, or simply love in return from the child.

"How about when a soldier falls on a grenade in a war and saves the rest of his platoon? Certainly that is unselfish." He answered that the soldier wanted glory more than life.

   "To get the full value of joy, you must have someone to divide it with."

—Mark Twain

"How about when a boy takes a girl out to dinner, buys her flowers and candy, pays for tickets to a movie or a concert? Certainly that is not selfish."

Again, Mr. Fortin replied by saying, "The boy is indeed selfish. He does all of that and then expects…." The teacher stopped talking, rolled his eyes, and smiled. I guess I knew what he was thinking.

My parents taught me not to be selfish and I didn't want to believe I was. However, Mr. Fortin refuted every example I could offer. It was difficult to accept the notion that people are selfish by nature. I knew people who were looking out for their own gain without any concern for others, but I also knew there were people who were always doing good things for others. I just didn't want to believe that everything I did was for my own benefit. I didn't want to believe that I was selfish along with everyone else.

Somewhere along the way, I realized that some people weigh the effects of a deed before they do it. If there are two or more possible results, they consistently choose the outcome that will give themselves the most in return. They totally disregard the dreams and desires of others. They are selfish. They don't like to share their tools, toys, or time. They don't give out recipes, formulas, or ideas. They are difficult to be around, unless you enjoy being victimized. Selfish people do not work well on teams, as their personal goals get in the way of the team's objectives. They seldom get the help they need to accomplish the things they cannot do on their own without manipulation of others.

On the other hand, some people tend to do things that not only benefit themselves but also significantly help others. The Wizard of Oz called them "Good Deed Doers." Individuals who carry this method of behavior to the extreme are called saints! The majority of these people are simply nice folks to be around. Although they may do what they do for their own good, they are not considered selfish.

Perhaps everything we do is done for our own good. However, only selfish people stop to contemplate their own gain before they act. *Selfless* people act and help others, knowing (subconsciously perhaps) that they will be rewarded later. When you think of it this way, people are not selfish when they pursue their own goals; rather, they are selfish when they ignore the goals of others.

❖ "Though I have all faith, so that I could remove mountains, and have not charity, I am nothing."

—First Corinthians.

When you set a goal that includes altruism, it means that you are trying to give more than you receive. It implies that the goal will help others as much or more than it will help yourself. This might appear counterproductive at first, especially if your goal is to *have* something. It doesn't make sense to give away more than you get in return. How can you move ahead if you are always losing ground? If your goal is to accumulate things, it makes more sense to try to obtain things by investing as little as possible. Cheap is good; free is better! Why pay more than you have to or give more than you get in return?

Altruism may not seem logical at first, especially since goals are typically designed to acquire material things. It is difficult to understand how altruism works to help reach a monetary goal. Would you give away more money than you receive in return? Would you trade a dollar for three quarters? Would you give money to a charity with which you have no connection? Would you give a poor stranger a fifty-dollar bill knowing that you might never see that person or the money again? You typically invest money where and when you are fairly sure you will see a return on your investment. Giving money away seems foolish and wasteful.

On the surface, altruism doesn't seem to apply to money, business, real estate, or other financial investments, but altruism doesn't mean throwing money away in bad investments. When investments are measured with money, they are made to get more than you give and the market dictates values. If stocks go down and you want to sell, you might get less than you put in no matter how unselfishly you made your investment. If a factory closes, real estate prices may plummet, and if you sell, you might receive less than you invested regardless of your good intentions. If diamonds become as plentiful as granite, prices could drop and leave you with pretty rocks instead of gems. Money invested purely to make more money does not guarantee a return. However, money given with altruism usually comes back multiplied.

Although altruism is about unselfish giving, it is also about getting. Altruism involves knowing (perhaps subconsciously) that when you give selflessly, you will always get something in return.

> "*A* bit of fragrance always clings to the hand that gives the rose."
> —*Chinese proverb* ❧

❧ "Charity sees the need not the cause."

—German proverb

Those who realize how altruism works know that it can be challenging to try to give more than you receive. When you know that what you give away will be returned multiplied, you might feel selfish giving anything away. Or you might be tempted to give whenever you feel a need to get. You might become selfishly selfless. But giving so that you can get is not what this is all about. Altruism does not involve manipulation because it is not necessary. To be truly altruistic, giving is done freely, with no strings attached and no expectations whatsoever.

Somewhere along the way, we forget that life is what we make of it. So often we want to get more out of life but are unwilling to put in anything more. Expecting to get more without giving more is like sitting in front of a field-stone fireplace waiting for dancing flames to appear and radiate heat. Fire is not magic. You have to put wood or gas into the fireplace before you can get light and warmth out of it. Only a fool would expect a warm fire without putting fuel in first. Likewise, only a fool sits around waiting to receive without first giving—and many do. You have to put energy into life before you get anything out and what you get out of life depends upon what you put in. As Earl Nightingale told me, "Our rewards in life will always be in direct proportion to our contributions." The more you put in, the more you will get out.

One of America's most successful business legends, W. Clement Stone, amassed great financial wealth through altruism. He lived by the credo that whatever you can conceive and believe is possible for you to achieve. He collaborated with Napoleon Hill, author of *Think and Grow Rich*, to produce and promote a philosophy for achievement and principles of success. Thousands of people have become rich because of reading their books and listening to their speeches. Stone knew how altruism worked and it made him millions. He was quoted as saying, "Be generous! Give to those you love; give to those who love you; give to the fortunate; give to the unfortunate—yes, give especially to those you don't want to give. You will receive abundance for your giving. The more you give, the more you will have!"

> *Investments in SMARTER goals that include altruism will yield dividends greater than any stock on Wall Street. They are inflation-proof and tax free.*

❖ "You have not done enough, you have never done enough, so long as it is still possible that you have something to contribute."

—Dag Hammarskjold

The primary reason people don't believe altruism works is that they have improper expectations. When they give someone a gift or do something nice for someone, they expect something back from that same person. When they do someone a favor, they expect a favor in return.

Somewhere along the way you have probably felt as if you gave and gave and gave and never got anything in return. You got tired of donating to every charity in town because no one donated to yours. You worked hard for your money and others should earn theirs, also. You always complimented others on the way they looked or the way they worked and you were disappointed because no one complimented you. When you feel this way, you have given with expectations. If you give expecting something in return, you are setting yourself up for disappointments.

With genuine, sincere altruism, there will be a return. There always is. There is no doubt about it. However, what comes back does not have to come directly from the person who received what you gave. It is important to realize that when you give freely, what you get in return may come from another source. It is a universal law. The rewards for selflessness are certain, although they may be delayed and they may come back to you via a direction and form you do not anticipate.

There are two things you can do if you give and do not get back what you feel you deserve:

1. Increase your giving. Remember the old adage: Don't give until it hurts. Give until it feels good. It only takes a little more.
2. Change the direction of your giving. What you are giving may be more beneficial to and appreciated by a different recipient.

Indirect goal achievement

It might appear that the shortest distance between where you are and where you want to be is a straight line, but that may not be the case. And you might think that the fastest way to get to your personal goal is to make sure every-

❧ "The greatest good you can do for another is not just to share your riches, but to reveal to him his own."

—Benjamin Disraeli

thing you do is directly related to accomplishing that goal for yourself, but that too may be wrong. The obvious route is not always the shortest or fastest.

Consider that on a flat map a trip from Los Angeles, California to London, England, would take you over most of the United States. On the curved sphere of the real earth, the shortest distance and the fastest route would take you over Canada, many miles to the north. Of course a perfectly straight line between Los Angeles and London would be through the crust of the earth, but that is not practical. Similarly, the shortest and fastest path to your goal is not always the obvious straight one.

The most effective way to attain your short-term goals is to work directly on them by yourself. But for long-term goals, that may not be the most efficient course. To fulfill your own personal dreams and aspirations, you may have to concern yourself with what others want. By helping others, you help yourself. To quote Ralph Waldo Emerson, "One of the most beautiful compensations in life is the fact that you cannot help another human being without helping yourself." As you help others, you help yourself and become stronger.

> "*Life's most persistent and urgent question is: What are you doing for others?*"
> —Martin Luther King, Jr. 🐾

You can advance directly toward your goal by yourself, or you can take a roundabout way by working to help others reach their goals. Rather than pursuing your goal using vertical thinking, taking objective steps toward your goal, you can choose a new, obscure course. Edward de Bono describes an alternate way of solving problems in his book *Lateral Thinking, Creativity Step by Step*. His ideas about handling information and restructuring insight offer ways to generate new ideas, alter paradigms, and create seemingly impossible solutions from seemingly irrelevant information. Implausible goals can become blatantly apparent when viewed after accomplishment.

Lateral thinking and altruism can make goal setting easier even if it looks more complicated at first. Helping others reach their goals can help you reach your own, especially when your goals are in similar directions.

🐾 "The best place to find a helping hand is at the end of your own arm."
—Swedish proverb

Helping others can generate synergy that yields achievements unattainable by any single individual. When your goals work in harmony with others and your lives are congruent, your efforts and accomplishments will increase exponentially.

> " *Y*ou will get everything you want when you help enough other people get what they want."
>
> —*Zig Zigler* ❧

If you have a dream to fulfill, it will come true faster if you can find out what other people want and help them secure their dreams. This often happens in marriages where one spouse supports the family while the other finishes a college program. It happens in business when employees help employers reach corporate goals and in turn reach their own. It happens in finance when an investor enables a business to produce a product and then later receives a return on the investment.

Altruism is giving when giving is not required

Giving things to others in a last will and testament could be seen as altruism, but that type of giving is not what I mean. Even though the document gives away your property when you die and distributes your assets without expectation of anything returning to you, this is not altruism. While the recipients will surely appreciate your generosity, you could realize the rewards of your wealth more if you gave it away while you were alive. Money is meant to be spent. Money is like manure. It doesn't do much until you spread it around. Death forces you to relinquish control of your property. Giving away your property when you die is just like paying taxes to the government. You have to do it. Forced giving is not altruism.

> " *I*s not dread of thirst when your well is full the thirst that is unquenchable? Give now that the season of giving be yours and not your inheritors."
>
> —*Kahlil Gibran* ❧

❧ "I don't take anything for depression. I give."

—Karen Johnson, RN

We have all heard the expression, "It is more blessed to give than to receive." I have always heard the word "blessed" in that adage pronounced with two syllables. Spoken with two syllables, bless-ed is an adjective meaning "holy." The expression implies that it is more sacred or saintly to be the giver than the recipient.

When I was a child I thought the expression meant that it was better to give than to get. That didn't make sense to me. I much preferred getting to giving. I didn't understand why anyone would want to give more than they got just to be holy. I thought it must be one of those spiritual laws adults wanted me to accept without question. Getting something usually made me happy. Giving things away was something I avoided, except for getting rid of old clothes or toys that didn't work any more.

Somewhere along the way I matured and learned about altruism, and I realized that by altering the pronunciation of the old expression a little, it made perfect sense. If "blessed" is pronounced with one syllable as the past tense of the verb "bless" (sometimes spelled "blest"), then the adage could be interpreted to mean we are more rewarded when we give than when we receive. The person doing the giving gets more than the person doing the receiving. The giver receives a blessing in return that is more valuable than that which was given. Simply put, you will be blessed with something when you give something away. That is altruism. He who gives, gets.

> "*It is better to do something without anything in return, than to miss a chance to do something good. You cannot do a kindness too soon, for you never know how soon it will be too late.*"
> —*Ralph Waldo Emerson* ❧

The idea of getting more by giving more is not new. Altruism is an ancient virtue that has been a part of every great society. An old Hindu proverb proclaims, "True happiness consists in making others happy." We all need to realize that the surest way to happiness for ourselves is to make sure those around us are happy.

❧ "We make a living by what we get. We make a life by what we give."
—Winston Churchill

Og Mandino explains the altruistic aspect of life in *A Better Way to Live*. "Extend to each person, no matter how trivial the contact, all the care and kindness and understanding and love that you can muster, and do it with no thought of any reward." Mandino knew that success is inevitable when you give more than you receive. "Today and every day, deliver more than you are getting paid to do. The victory of success will be half won when you learn the secret of putting out more than is expected in all that you do."

Altruism is also about charity

Charity involves giving for the good of the community. Even if you believe that people don't deserve your help, you shouldn't miss an opportunity to do someone a favor or perform a benevolent deed, even when you know there will be no gratitude. By helping your neighbors and those who are in need, you build better communities and strengthen your own personal character. Be ready to give whenever you have the chance. Opportunities to be altruistic abound.

There is no material *thing* you can give away without diminishing your own supply. If you give me a dollar, I have one more and you have one less. If you have a dollar and I have a dollar and we exchange, you still have one and I still have one. But what you give does not have to be a thing. Things like money don't multiply as easily as thoughts. If you have an idea and I have a different idea and we exchange, then we both have two. We each have more than before. Because we both have two, there is likely to be synergy between us that will create a third idea, which will be greater than the sum of the two.

> "*You give but little when you give of your possessions. It is when you give of yourself that you truly give.*"
> —*Kahlil Gibran*

Altruism is about giving and making investments without lessening what you have. Even prehistoric people realized that you cannot hold a torch to light

"No one has ever become poor by giving."

—Anne Frank

> "*I will smile at friend and foe alike and make every effort to find, in him or her, a quality to praise, now that I realize the deepest yearning of human nature is the craving to be appreciated.*"
>
> —Og Mandino ❖

another's path without brightening your own. Father James Keller, founder of the Christophers, used to say, "A candle loses nothing by lighting another candle." By helping others, you help yourself and never diminish what you have.

Give what you have to give while you have the chance. You are in a unique position to make a difference as a parent, an employee, or a friend. Your time, talents, and attention are gifts that are hard to measure and impossible to assess. Give what only you can give and what you are good at giving.

The painter gives the world a portrait. The sculptor gives a statue. The musician gives a tune. The poet gives rhyme. The writer gives words and ideas. The actor gives a performance. If you are artistically challenged and feel you have nothing worthy to give, you still can. The most altruistic art, the art of giving pleasure, requires only the desire to do so.

There are other things that can be given often and easily.

- Give supportive encouragement. Applaud performance.
- Give more recognition. Praise appropriate behavior.
- Give credit where credit is due. Honor accomplishments.
- Give appreciation. Find the good in all you see.
- Give compliments. Little comments may be appreciated more than any thing given as a gift.
- Give kind words.
- Give time.

> "*In this world, you must be a bit too kind to be kind enough.*"
>
> —Pierre Carlet de Chamblain de Marivaux ❖

Volunteer and donate your energy to organizations and philanthropic projects. Consider joining a service club like Habitat for Humanity, Rotary International, Kiwanis, Lions, Optimist Club, Elks, Jaycees, or Special Olympics.

Become a member or leader of a youth group like the Scouts, 4-H, Junior Achievement, Big Brothers and Big Sisters, or an organization in your local schools. Lend a hand to the elderly by talking or walking with them, reading to them, or playing bingo. Join a professional organization. Help out with fundraisers or solicitations for the March of Dimes, Heart Association, Cancer Society, or United Way. Or get active in one of the many religious groups that aid the homeless, needy, and unfortunate. Churches, synagogues, mosques, and the like offer opportunities to give and help others.

> *"It ill becomes us to invoke in our daily prayers the blessings of God, the Compassionate, if we in turn will not practice elementary compassion towards our fellow creatures."*
> —*Mahatma Gandhi*

- Give out smiles.
  As you progress along your path through life, give everyone you see one of your smiles and you will leave miles of smiles behind you. Realize that people who receive your warm greetings won't always smile back at you. But somewhere along the way a smile will be returned to brighten a gloomy day for you.
- Give love.
  Decades ago, Miss Wisconsin made a profound statement during the pageant when she became Miss America. I remember her talking about a story in the Bible when Jesus fed 5,000 people with only two fishes and five loaves of bread. "Love is like that," she said. "It doesn't begin to multiply until you start giving it away."
- Give knowledge.
  Share what you have learned. You may want to give out copies of this book if you feel the ideas will help others.

Altruism means being unselfish even though everything you do might be done subconsciously for

> *"Too often we underestimate the power of a touch, a smile, a kind word, a listening ear, an honest compliment, or the smallest act of caring, all of which have the potential to turn a life around."*
> —*Leo Buscaglia* ❧

"*This is the miracle that happens every time to those who really love; the more they give, the more they possess.*"
—*Rainer Maria Rilke* ❧

yourself. Pick up trash and litter even when it's not yours just because it makes you feel good to make the world look better. Plant a tree that you will never sit under just because you like to create shade and freshen the air for everyone. Let someone get ahead of you in traffic or in line just to be nice. What could delay your advancement by seconds could assure your safe arrival.

Think of the goals of others when you set your goals to be something. Think of what you can give and you will get whatever you need.

Those who are truly successful know that *SMARTER goals* are altruistic.

 *Reasonably balanced*

Somewhere along the way, we need to realize that *SMARTER Success* can be achieved by setting goals that are reasonably balanced.

If you are like me, you occasionally find it difficult to balance your life. Your family, career, health, finances, social life, and religion are all very important and require your attention, but how can you distribute your efforts evenly? Balancing a life can be challenging, especially when your life is complicated and complex.

When your family includes children and a spouse, you may have to balance:

- finding time for helping with homework.
- bathing and dressing the children.
- hauling kids to lessons and practices.
- attending competitions and events.
- giving attention to your partner.
- doing chores and housework.
- finding time for hobbies.
- and if your mom or dad is alive, being a parent to a parent.

When your budget includes a large mortgage payment, you may have to balance:

- your checkbook.
- worrying about money.
- arguing about money.
- credit card debt.
- part-time jobs.
- a job layoff.

When your health includes a physical condition or disease, you may have to balance:

- medications and therapies.
- vitamins and supplements.
- diet and exercise.
- your weight and appetite.
- obsessions or addictions.

When you have a career, you may have to balance:

- travel away from home.
- hours at the office or on the job.
- continuing education.
- on-call time and phone calls at home.
- swing shifts.
- graveyard shifts and sleeping days.
- obligations to professional organizations.

When you have an active social life, you may have to balance:

- time with friends.
- giving parties, dinners, etc.
- going to parties, dinners, etc.
- involvement with civic organizations.
- attending meetings.

When you have spiritual convictions and belong to an organized religion, you may have to balance:

- attending worship services.
- tithing of time and money.

- volunteer work.
- committee work.
- evangelism.

In addition to the objectives listed above, you may have to balance:

- your sleep, rest, and activity.
- your dreams and disappointments.
- your pleasure and recreation.
- finding time to be alone with yourself.

And someone has to take care of the pets.

With so many obligations and commitments pulling you in different directions, it is unreasonable to believe you can balance everything perfectly all of the time. There are always distractions and complications that will throw your life out of balance if you let them. To balance your goals and objectives *reasonably* is the best that you can do.

One of the first things you can do to create reasonably balanced goals and hence, a balanced life, is to stop and assess your present situation. Is your life currently out of balance? How bad is it?

Do you have children, and if you do, can you remember their names and ages?

Do you have a spouse, and if you do, how long has it been since you renewed your courtship by going on a date or doing the things you originally did to attract your spouse?

Do you have enough money to meet your needs? How about your wants?

Do you have financial debt, and if you do, is it at the lowest possible interest rate and secured with enough (or any) collateral?

Are you healthy with a normal weight for your height?

Do you eat a balanced diet on a regular schedule?

Do you have any obsessions or addictions?

Are you working for a living or living for your work?

How much of your day is spent working for money?

How much of your week is spent with friends?

How much of your month is spent involved with civic or professional organizations?

How much of your time is spent in self-development?

How much of your life is spent in spiritual reflection, worship, and devotion?
Do you have a pet, and if you do, do you realize someone has to feed and
care for it?

It is easy to get focused on one goal in life and neglect others. If you concentrate on a relationship or a career, you might ignore your finances or
family. Working too hard for money can take time away from your relationships, family, and health. Social activities can be more attractive than religious obligations and induce you to party instead of pray. With so many
goals and responsibilities, it is common and normal for your life to get out of
balance.

I have never met a person who has a perfectly balanced life. Mine isn't. I
have never been able to do all the things I wanted or needed to do. I have tried
to do the important things when they needed to be done, but I am sure I neg-
lected many along the way.

To get into veterinary school, I needed to focus most of my energy on
studying. I maintained friendships but never committed to marriage until
after I graduated. Then I believed I needed to focus most of my energy on
starting a veterinary practice. I maintained a marriage, but never annulled
the previous marriage to my business. My weight climbed to 220 pounds—
fifty more than what it should have been. I drank a little more alcohol than I
needed and I smoked tobacco for a short time. Sixty-hour workweeks were
common and I dropped out of most civic, religious, and professional organizations. Somewhere along the way, my wife filed for divorce. Although my life
never completely toppled over, I discovered what it was like to live a life that
was really out of balance.

Balancing focus and energy—the airplane analogy

To get an airplane off the ground, a pilot must push the engines to full
throttle. Full power is needed to accelerate the plane and create enough lift
for the plane to rise into the air. However, once the plane is in the air, the pilot
must back off on the throttle and allow the engines to slow down. If the
engines stayed wide open for very long, they would burn out.

If you pursue goals that are challenging and difficult, you may have to
behave like the pilot and the plane. It might take all the focused energy you
can produce to get your project going, but once you get it off the ground you

risk burnout if you don't back off on the energy you are expending. There are other similarities between flying a plane and living a life.

Before you take off on an adventure, you need to create a flight plan, which is like setting a goal in life. Then you need to check out the mechanics of the plane, which is like making sure you are physically fit. You must check your fuel, making sure it is pure and powerful, like the food you need to eat. When you are seated in the plane, you must fasten your seatbelt. Likewise in life, you need to take precautions and security measures for rough times—your future might not always be smooth.

When the checklist is completed, you start the engine, recheck the gauges, and begin to taxi to the runway. Here you rev the engine and eventually take off. However, the direction of the departure is not necessarily your choice. Runways and winds at airports dictate the direction in which you will take off. Once you get off the ground you need to reset your heading (direction) for your desired destination.

Realize that much of the time during a flight you will not be headed directly toward your goal. Due to winds and weather patterns, your plane may be off course a lot of the time. You may expedite your trip and make it safer by going around thunderstorms or violent weather. Likewise, you may not always be headed directly toward your own goals. Delays and detours may alter your course, in which case you must readjust your direction accordingly.

The length of time you can stay up in the air will depend upon many factors, but eventually you will need to land. Takeoffs are optional but landings are mandatory. Planes need to be refueled and maintained, and it is much easier to repair them when they land by intention. Landing your life means resting or sleeping and refueling your subconscious energy reserves to restore your vitality. Flying isn't dangerous. Crashing is. Don't fall from the sky because you forgot to refuel. Plan to take breaks, refresh yourself, and maintain your balance along the way.

The lesson to learn about pursuing a goal from the airplane analogy is that it sometimes takes all the power you have to get started toward a goal. When you do, it is essential to cut back on the energy you are putting into your goal and reassess your position and direction. Take a look at all of your other goals that may need attention and then balance your energy.

Some people make a great takeoff for a goal and then lose control. They put unbelievable energy into a project, speed down the runway, soar into the sky, go too high, and zip right off into the stratosphere like space cadets. They lose sight of their other goals. Eventually, they burn out, go into a dive, and crash. To prevent that from happening, it is essential that you attempt to balance your efforts for your family, career, health, relationship, financial, and spiritual goals.

Remember that with SMARTER goals, the destination is established only to determine your direction. Success involves not so much what is at the end of the journey as your attitude along the way. And your attitude will determine your altitude—how close you come to your goal at the top. The higher you get, the more balance you need. Keep your goals reasonably balanced so you don't fall on the way to the top.

The balance of nature

Balance is universal in nature and is a natural phenomenon. I first learned about the balance of nature in fifth-grade music class. My teacher introduced me to a new repetitive song about a woman who swallowed a fly. As I remember the words, it went something like this: "There was an old woman who swallowed a fly. It wrickled and ickled and tickled inside her. I don't know why she swallowed the fly. I guess she'll die."

The song goes on to tell the story with rhythm and rhyme. The old woman swallowed a spider to go after the fly. Then she swallowed a bird to catch the spider. That was absurd. Then she swallowed a cat to catch the bird and a dog to catch the cat. A goat almost got stuck in her throat trying to get the dog. Finally she swallowed a horse. Poor old woman, she died, of course. Little did my music class teacher realize that she had given me a lesson in biology. The old woman swallowed each creature to get another creature. I learned that all animals have natural predators. All animals live at the expense of other lives.

It sounds cruel that animals must kill to live, but that is how nature keeps animal populations in check. It is the balance of nature. To keep animals from getting out of balance with their natural food resources, nature has a system of checks and balances that provides predator animals to control prey populations. It is unsettling to think that animals as cute and harmless as little bunnies will be killed and consumed, but that is the way nature works. There are parts of nature that we find objectionable; yet, without balance, animals would starve or face equally miserable fates.

Learning to balance is natural

Babies born to wild animals are often easy prey for wild predators. Therefore, they must be hidden by their mother, carried by an adult, or in the case of larger animals like deer, moose, and elk, they must be able to get up and move on their own shortly after birth. If they don't, they die. Likewise, large domestic animals like cattle, hogs, and horses—which once ran wild—give birth to babies that have surprisingly strong bones and muscles. A colt or a filly can stand and walk within minutes after being born. The antics of new foals are comical as their long spindly legs spread out to the sides. Their limbs become tangled and twisted, causing the foals to stumble over their own feet. Once they stand, the comedy continues as the babies try to find a nipple from which to nurse. In order to survive, large animals learn quickly to get up, get balanced, and run.

A human baby is completely dependent upon its parents. The skeleton of the newborn human is soft, which affords poor support for the baby's body but makes the birthing process easier for the mother. When the bones become firm and the muscles strengthen, the baby stands, wobbles, and eventually walks. Human babies can be just as comical to watch as they learn to walk. And their entertainment value sometimes lasts for months as they practice and become coordinated enough to walk steadily.

Whether it takes hours or months to learn to balance and walk, practice makes for improvement. Even though the little ones fall often, they get back up and keep trying. Before long they learn to balance their bodies and walk without aid.

Balancing goals can be learned just the way you learned to balance your body. At one time you couldn't even walk, but with practice and patience you built yourself up so that walking became effortless and easy. Most likely you also learned to balance your body on a bike and maybe even on a unicycle, stilts, or a tightrope. With practice and patience, you can also balance your goals effortlessly.

Balancing your family, health, career, relationship, financial, and spiritual goals is a little like a juggler who keeps six balls in the air at a time. The juggler actually throws the balls up one at a time and catches them individually. He switches contact and control from ball to ball so quickly it appears that the six balls are being handled simultaneously.

It isn't easy to juggle balls, batons, rings, or blocks unless you practice, practice, practice. Although some people are born with an aptitude for juggling, most anyone can learn to juggle with enough practice. A master juggler makes it look easy because of years of experience and practice.

Juggling goals and priorities in life can be just as challenging as juggling material objects. You need to focus on each individual area and yet be aware of all the others. You might want to start with balancing just a few goals while postponing some for a while. It gets easier with practice, so don't get discouraged if you drop a ball when you are learning to handle multiple goals and objectives. Even the best jugglers drop one now and then.

Of course, if you don't try to juggle—if you simply hold the balls in your hands—there is very little risk of dropping any. But just as a professional juggler isn't very interesting while holding things still, life is uninteresting if you don't take risks and make things happen. If you don't have a family, if you don't have a job, if you don't create friendships and commitments, and if you don't ponder spirituality, you probably don't have much to balance—or to keep you awake!

How to balance your life by integrating your goals

Once you establish the possibility that you could do better at balancing your life, you must decide what goals need to be adjusted and how you can balance your time and energy. No one can do two things at exactly the same time, but when things are done very closely together they appear to be simultaneous.

Have you ever seen an entertainer spin dishes on top of long sticks? Being an expert at balancing objects, the person puts a plate on top of a stick, spins the plate, then wiggles the stick to get it going very fast. The process is then repeated with another plate. When the plates spin quickly, they are very stable and balanced. As they slow down, they begin to wobble. The juggler must start plates while watching for spinning plates that need more stick wiggling to rev them up before they fall. When all the plates are spinning, the person makes sure each plate gets the attention it needs so all the plates stay on their sticks as long as possible.

Just as the juggler balances all the plates, you can work on many goals simultaneously and yet give each the attention it needs if the goals you set are related and are in harmony with each other. This type of juggling is called goal integration. Goal integration is a system of multi-tasking that aligns goals so that work on one will also advance the others. By working and planning to integrate your goals, your goals become congruent and you eliminate conflict between your aspirations and your efforts. If all of your goals keep you moving in the same general direction and your activities are well integrated, your life can be reasonably balanced.

Balanced goals complement the reach for each other.

The classic family dairy farm is a good example of goal integration. A husband and wife work together to raise children who help with the chores. The work is strenuous but everybody eats fresh, wholesome food. The animal products that they produce are sold to pay the mortgage on the farm and to provide personal needs and things for the home. The family gets together daily for dinner, meets with the neighbors on Friday or Saturday, and devotes one day a week to religion. The goals for the family, for health, finances, careers, social relations, and religion are pursued at the same time and goals are reasonably balanced.

Many other lifestyles can be balanced just as reasonably; however, most are not. Parents work in separate businesses. Children are involved in sports, clubs, and after-school activities. Jobs require less physical exertion and food is processed and preserved. Wants outweigh income and debt extends beyond assets. Relationships increase in number yet decrease in quality. There tends to be conflict among goals. Balance becomes challenging when there are so many things to do, deadlines to meet, and obligations to fulfill.

Multi-tasking can help if you make sure the things you are doing are always congruent with your major goals in life. Most of us can walk and chew gum at the same time. We can whistle while we work. Some of us can simultaneously drive a car, talk on a cell phone, drink a beverage, and write notes to ourselves while opening and reading the mail at 55 mph. (I am probably not the only veterinarian who has done all this between farm visits on rarely used country roads. Even when there is no traffic, it is a dangerous practice and I do not advise anyone to multitask like this while driving.) We can watch the morning news on television or listen to audiotapes while running on a treadmill. We can care for children, clean the house, make dinner, and help with homework while planning a vacation. We can write notes to friends while waiting at the doctor's office or the car repair shop. We can pursue our goals simultaneously if we work at it.

You are what you eat

Consider your health when balancing your goals. Americans are obsessed with eating, but so is almost everyone else in the world. People need to eat. Unfortunately, our society is really into overeating. We eat so much that obesity is now a major medical problem that increases the average person's risk of heart disease, diabetes, and cancer. The quantity, quality, and method of consumption of our food have a direct impact on the condition of our health. The day will come when a physician who does not inquire about the diet of a patient will be guilty of malpractice.

The word diet connotes a special array of foods. If you are on a diet, it usually means you are eating certain foods for a special, specific reason. Nutritionists create diets to help balance the needs of your body, but those needs are not always known. The controversy over exactly what you should or should not eat is demonstrated by the fact that new diets are sold and marketed every week. There are diets:

...to lose weight.
...to gain weight.
...to regulate diabetes.
...to alleviate allergies.
...to regulate blood pressure.
...to help with constipation.
...to heal ulcers.
...to clear up skin conditions.
...to relieve anxiety.
...and to cure just about any other ailment.

Veterinarians already consider it standard practice to scrutinize the diet of patients when assessing illness or health maintenance. The primary way a farmer can tell that a cow is sick is to note that she is not eating. One of the first signs a pet owner notices when a pet gets sick is that the little animal leaves the food dish full. Appetite is often the first thing to go when an animal becomes ill. Veterinarians must always inquire about the patient's diet because it plays a big part in maintaining health and in causing disease.

People spend surprisingly large amounts of money on diets that promise to undo what has occurred due to simple overeating. Some diets encourage eating more protein. Some say eat more carbohydrates. Some say eat more often. Some say take supplements, while some advocate eating special herbs and extracts.

The food pyramid that is promoted by the USDA and the Beef Council is a good start for balancing a diet. According to Dr. Walter C. Willet's book, *Eat, Drink, and Be Healthy*, the pyramid needs a little adjustment and improvements should be made. But the diet of most individuals is so far from the pyramid that it would be a good model to follow until what is eaten gets a bit closer to being balanced. There is no point to fine-tuning a diet until you are at least close to the right channel.

It takes time and effort to organize your life so that your goals for your family, career, health, finances, relationships, and spiritual beliefs are reasonably balanced, congruent, and integrated. When they are, your efforts in one area will not hinder others and you can endeavor to reach all of them simultaneously.

Those who are truly successful know that SMARTER goals are reasonably balanced.

Timeless

Somewhere along the way, we need to realize that *SMARTER Success* can be achieved by setting goals that are timeless.

> *The dictionary defines "timeless" as "having no beginning and no end." As I use it in this book, timeless means "without end," as all goals obviously need to have beginnings.*

*T*here are two dates on a traditional graveyard headstone—one recording the day of your birth, the other your death. The significance of your life is determined by how you spend the time between those two dates.

Time is the one thing you can spend like Bill Gates, Warren Buffett, or any other billionaire. You can invest your time working or playing or thinking or sleeping or doing nothing. To get the greatest return from your time on earth, you must invest your time wisely. Chances are Gates and Buffett do that often.

> "*T*his time, like all times, is a very good one, if we but know what to do with it."
> —*Ralph Waldo Emerson* 🐾

Maybe times are too rough right now. Now is not the right time to set goals. But *now* is the only time you can control. Now is the time to think about what you want to *have* and what you want to *be*. Thinking about goals may mean devoting some of your limited time today, but it can save you days or even years in the future.

> "*In times like these, it helps to recall that there have always been times like these.*"
> —Paul Harvey ❧

Middle-aged and elderly people tell me that they are too old to set new goals. The opportunities they had when they were young are no longer available. Some will say that goal setting doesn't work anymore. Things aren't like they were back in the good old days. This may all be true. Certainly things have changed. But when things are averaged out, they are neither better nor worse than they have ever been. Of course, your opinion about different eras will depend upon your personal experiences, attitude, and perspective.

A poet by the name of Ovid wrote, "Let others praise ancient times; I am glad I was born in these." He realized that the current time is the best time because it is the only time in which *you* are living. He knew that the past had not always been as wonderful as it was remembered. He also knew that the time in which he lived would someday be considered ancient. The idea that the good old days were better than today is not new. Ovid's quote was made over two thousand years ago in the year 81 B.C.

> "*The illusion that times that were are better than those that are has probably pervaded all ages.*"
> —Horace Greeley ❧

It's not unusual to look back at your childhood and wish you were younger or that you could live it over again. It's not unusual to believe that previous generations had better times. It's not unusual to wish you lived in another time, either the past or the future. However, until time travel becomes a reality, the present is the only time in which you can live. Now is the only time you may choose a path and influence your future.

Norman Cousins wrote, "Time given to thought is the greatest time saver." He experienced a connection between his thoughts and a very serious illness. When twenty-six aspirin and twelve phenylbutazone tablets a day did not relieve his pain, he discovered that ten minutes of genuine belly

> "*We want to live in the present, and the only history worth a tinker's damn is the history we make today.*"
> —*Henry Ford* ❧

laughter worked as an anesthetic that would allow him a couple of hours of pain-free sleep. His book, *Anatomy of an Illness: As Perceived by the Patient* is his recounting of doctors and hospitals and his struggle with a crippling disease in which he refused to be a passive observer.

Norman Cousins' research on his own condition, as well as his review of many medical journals, revealed that people who think happy thoughts are healthier. He demonstrated that time spent thinking can and does alter health. He suggested that laughter could actually help a body heal. If you stop to think about it, it's hard to be sick and laugh at the same time. Being sick is a great waste of time. Because thinking influences health, taking time to think about being happy and healthy can actually save you time being sick later in life. Thinking can often influence health more than any pill or procedure.

When is the right time to start thinking about setting goals? Maybe the timing is not right at this point in your life to reach for your dreams. Maybe you just don't have time to think about your future plans. Maybe you just don't have time to write out your goals. Maybe you want to delay setting goals until:

…you are a little older.

…you are married.

…the kids are out of the house.

…the kids finish school.

…next summer, next fall, next winter, or next spring.

…the car loan is paid off.

…the mortgage is satisfied.

…you get divorced.

…you lose a few pounds.

…you retire.

Or maybe you will put off your dreams until you die!

Taking time to think about goals and what you really want greatly increases your chances of creating a successful life and developing your full potential. Whether your goal is to be a respectable parent or a child, a loving spouse or a loyal friend, a dedicated employee or benevolent employer, or just to be happy and healthy, you need time to think about what you should do to accomplish your goals. Time spent making plans and creating a course of action will produce a better, more secure journey toward your goals, whatever they are. Time spent in preparation makes a task easier to accomplish. As Abe Lincoln is credited with saying, "If I had two hours to fell a tree, I would spend the first thirty minutes sharpening the axe."

There may be no better time than the present to alter your path and design your destiny. Time management experts say, "Plan your work and then work your plan." If you don't, you might end up someplace you would rather not be. Working for things that do not give you satisfaction wastes time that could be invested in activities that produce lasting success, happiness, and health.

Time is relative

When people say we all have the same amount of time in a day, I respectfully disagree. Time does not move at the same pace for all people. It moves faster for some people and slower for others.

A simple experiment helps illustrate the idea that time passes at different rates for different people. The youth group to which I belonged when I was about ten years old had monthly meetings with parents and children. Our leader was always challenged to provide activities that were appropriate for adults and children alike. One game we played had to do with time. The leader asked everyone to sit on chairs in two semi-circles, one behind the other in the middle of our meeting room. Parents were seated behind their respective children. The leader asked everyone to stand and then he explained the game.

He asked all the participants to close their eyes and pledge not to open them until the end of the game. No one was to say anything or make any noises. When the leader gave the signal, everyone was to start thinking about the passage of time. When an individual believed one minute of time had elapsed, he or she was to sit down. The leader would watch the clock and the participants. The one who sat down closest to the one-minute mark on the clock was the winner of the game.

This simple game made me realize that time is often difficult to determine without a clock. At our meeting, I was out of the contest early. Most of my comrades sat down after twenty seconds or so. One kid and two adults sat down after the one-minute mark. Nobody in the audience of forty people knew exactly when one minute had gone by. Without some type of timing device—a clock, stopwatch, or sand running through an hourglass—we could not be certain about the time.

> *Anyone who has lived in a family household knows the length of one minute depends upon which side of the bathroom door you're on.*

If you ask the folks in a nursing home about the passage of time and then ask the employees at a publishing house the same question, you will get very different answers. One group passes the time of day playing games, doing crafts, or simply sitting and watching the world go by. The other group scurries to meet deadlines for manuscript delivery, proofreading, layout, design, printing, and all the other details required to get a newspaper, magazine, or book produced on time. The two groups regard time very differently because time is relative to what they are doing.

Albert Einstein proved his theory of general relativity mathematically with volumes of notes and calculations. Einstein's complex theory can be reduced to one equation: $E = MC^2$. The formula is simple, but it is not very easy to understand. It states scientifically that time is not always constant. Time is relative to the environment in which it is measured. Time is relative to speed when the frame of reference is changing as in a spaceship traveling near the speed of light. For the most part, this is difficult for us to understand when everything moves with us through space at similar speeds. When Einstein was asked to put his theory of time relativity into simple terms, he supposedly explained it like this, "When a young man sits with a pretty girl for an hour, it seems like a minute. But let him sit on a hot stove for a minute, and it's longer than any hour. That's relativity."

Although your observations of time may not be as scientific as Einstein's, you know from your own experiences that time flows at different rates. When you are having a good time with your friends, time flies. When you are stuck with people you dislike, time can drag on and on. When you are sick or bored, time can pass very slowly. When you are tired and lie down to sleep, you can awaken eight hours later and feel as though you had dozed off for just minutes.

There are ways to get more out of the usual twenty-four hours in a day. Most people sleep eight hours a night—some more, some less. If you work at it, you can sleep more efficiently. You may think at first that working at sleeping sounds ridiculous. Sleep should be relaxation and leisure, not work. Indeed, sleep should be rest. However, if you don't completely relax and clear your mind of the problems and pressures of the day, you may spend hours restlessly tossing and turning. To sleep better, you can go to bed and make an effort to get a refreshing rest instead of just waiting for sleep to overtake your conscious thoughts. You can really work at getting better sleep.

This is a technique I use to get eight hours of sleep in six hours of time. First, I totally relax the skeletal muscles of my body, starting with my toes and working up through my legs, torso, arms, neck, face, and scalp. When everything is relaxed to a point where I no long feel the presence of my body, I think of the color white and clear my conscious mind. I am not sure what I do next because I have always entered a deep, rejuvenating state of sleep by this point in the procedure. By sleeping more efficiently, I free up time in which I can accomplish more of my goals. Even on days when I intend to do nothing, I can wake up early and be ready to get a good start.

Another place you can maximize your efforts and get a little more time is by taking a nap or break when you get tired. You can take a quick fifteen-minute nap and then return to work revitalized and refreshed. (It is important to make sure the people you work with know in advance what you are doing.) A catnap makes your work time more efficient than it would be without the rest break. The genius inventor, Thomas Edison, supposedly had a bed in his laboratory where he would sleep short periods of time and then work around the clock on his inventions.

Perhaps your job is too important to allow for a short nap. Perhaps you just don't have the time to stop and clear your mind and ponder important decisions. Perhaps there is no way you can set aside time for meditation without being interrupted by phone calls or interactions with family members or fellow workers. Maybe your life is more complicated than that of Mahatma Gandhi, who regularly found time for rest and rejuvenation. He reportedly set aside a whole day for meditation once a week. That made the rest of his week more productive. Of course Mahatma Gandhi might not have been as busy as you are. He was just the father of modern India—the second most populated country in the world.

There is yet another way you can maximize the time you have. Time is a valuable commodity and you can use it more wisely if you don't engage in negative activities. When you are trying to fix the blame, you are wasting time that could be spent fixing the problem. When you express negative emotions like resentment, jealousy, revenge, and hatred, you are wasting precious moments that could be invested in positive goals. Because you waste time thoughtlessly being negative, you may find yourself neglecting to do what is really important. You run out of time and utilize the most abused excuse for not reaching goals—"I just don't have time."

There is a time when every second counts and a time to ignore the clock

Animals don't pay much attention to clocks, but they can tell time. Cows know when it is time to be milked. A standard dairy practice is to milk cows every ten to twelve hours. If you hang around a farm for awhile, you will observe that the cows line up by the barn or milking parlor twice a day without human supervision. They seem to know when it is time for milking, almost as if they were watching a clock. But of course they are not, and you can prove this easily by observing cows when clocks change in the spring and fall for daylight savings time. The cows stay on their same routine and are one hour early or late for milking, depending upon which way the clocks have been adjusted.

Birds return to feeders at the same time daily. Squirrels become active in the mornings at about the same time every day. Most pets will let their owners know when it is feeding time. Even without clocks, animals observe the sun, internal bio-clocks, and variations in body function (milk production, hunger, hormone levels, etc.) and gauge the passage of time.

As in any profession, time can be very important in veterinary medicine. On several occasions I have been called to a dairy farm because a cow ruptured a mammary vein. Mammary veins are large blood vessels that run along each side of high-producing dairy cows from the udder (mammary glands) to the chest. The veins are larger in diameter than a garden hose and are located just under the skin on each side of the cow's belly. The vessels are commonly called milk veins, but they do not carry milk to the udder as the name might imply. When a really big cow gets up, she sometimes places her foot so close to the trunk of her body that she actually steps on some of her own skin. As she rises, the skin can get caught under the foot. It usually snaps free as her body rises higher and most of the time it is not a big problem. However, if that little bit of skin just happens to be over the mammary vein, and if there is enough friction and force, the foot can put a little hole in the skin and in the blood vessel. That causes a leak in the vein and blood squirts out rapidly.

Because the blood vessel is low on the animal's body, there is a lot of pressure in it. Even a little hole can spurt lots of blood in a small amount of time. A 1,400-pound dairy cow can bleed to death in a matter of minutes when a mammary vein is punctured. If the bleeding can be stopped soon enough (usually by suturing the side of the vein closed), the cow can survive. In the case of a ruptured mammary vein, time is of the essence. Veterinarians must know this. Timing can make the difference between saving a milk-producing cow's life or recommending that she take a trip to the butcher shop. In a case like this, time is extremely important.

In other cases, time heals wounds better than any medicine or procedure. Some problems are better off if you let nature take its course. Obviously time is not what actually heals a wound, but animals need time to mend wounds. Some lacerations or cuts on dogs can be closed with a surgery while under anesthesia in an animal hospital, or the same wound might heal just as nicely with time, naturally. Veterinarians need to know when to let a patient lick a wound and when it is time to close the wound surgically.

Before a veterinarian can practice medicine and surgery, most state governments require him or her to pass a competency test and be licensed. States administer examinations only to qualified applicants who are graduates of accredited veterinary colleges. The long tests are mostly written, but at one time it was common for examining boards to administer verbal examinations. The veterinary examiner who was assigned to me when I applied for a license asked me a question something like this:

If three different farm clients called one veterinarian at about the same time, which patient should the veterinarian attend to first?

1. A heifer (a young female cow) in labor trying to give birth to her first calf.
2. An older cow that is bloating with gas in its stomach.
3. A horse that is bleeding.

The answers to this question are not always the same, but a verbal answer accompanied by supportive reasons gives the examiner an impression of the applicant's knowledge and common sense concerning veterinary practice. It also reveals the new doctor's abilities in the area of triage.

Triage is a system designed to derive the greatest benefit from a limited commodity. In veterinary practice it refers to time, medicines, treatment facilities, and procedures that are not sufficient for all of the patients that may need help. Attention is first given to those who may survive with immediate care. It is denied or delayed to those who are certain to die or to those who will likely live without any help.

With more information, triage can be performed with more precision and efficiency. In the scenario concerning the heifer, the cow, and the horse, it would be nice to know if the heifer had just started to labor or if she had already been straining for most of the day. A heifer that is trying to deliver her first calf needs more time for her birth canal to stretch and open up compared with an older cow. Some farmers get overanxious and call the veterinarian for assistance too soon. As a joke, one old vet once told me that the only reason you should hurry to a heifer calving is so that you get there before she pushes it out on her own, in which case you can't charge for delivering the calf.

It would be helpful to know more about the cow with the stomach problems. A cow with foaming or gas bloat can die from suffocation in minutes due to the increased pressure in her stomach. Cows have four stomachs, and the first one can hold as much as fifty gallons. The bloated stomach can push on the cow's diaphragm and ribs and make her abdomen so big and tight that she cannot breathe. She may need to have a hose passed through her throat and into the stomach to let off the pressure. She might need to have a hole made in her side through the skin and into the stomach to let off the gas quickly. On the other hand, if the cow can simply burp or belch, the pressure can be relieved without human help.

More information is also needed about the horse that is hemorrhaging. When someone reports that a horse is bleeding it may mean several things. A little cut that drips a drop of blood every two minutes will eventually stop on its own, but in the meantime it can get an owner very excited. Bleeding could also mean a major artery is spurting and that pints of blood are being lost. Of course, all bleeding eventually stops, but it is rather important to the animal that the bleeding stops before the heart does.

There are other factors that enter into the triage question above. What are the distances to and between the farms? How long will it take to get from one farm to another? Can any of the owners be advised to give first aid to their animal until the veterinarian can arrive to help? Do any of the clients owe money to the veterinary practice or do they intend to ask for free service? *Pro bono* work, free service for the good of the public, is beneficial for society, but it hurts the financial status of a business when it is in excess. A veterinarian should not be greedy, but profit makes it possible to stay in business and offer needed services to those who do pay their bills.

With a little stretch of the meaning, you can triage time in your own life—allot time first to the activities that will produce the greatest benefit. Some activities are clearly urgent and necessary. Others are certainly a waste of time. Some activities occupy a nebulous region in between. Just as medical triage needs information to be done intelligently, you can allocate your time better when you have more information. To use your time wisely, it is important to think about what you are doing with your time, and give enough time to what you think is really important, not just what seems to be urgent.

Time is important when your goal is to have something

Failure to reach a goal in a given amount of time can be a major source of depression and poor self-image. A psychiatrist told me that the frustration that develops if goals are not met on time could lead to serious mental illness. He implied that goal setting only works for those who consistently reach their goals. He suggested that goals not be set too high, if they are set at all, so that they can be accomplished easily. His comments made sense if goals with deadlines are set to *have* things. He didn't realize that there are two kinds of goals—to *have* something or to *be* something.

When your goal is to *have* something, time is of the essence. A deadline for completion of the goal sets a time by which you will fulfill your dream. Self-imposed deadlines can provide substantial motivation. A time limit for a goal can induce urgency and promote accomplishment. With this type of goal, gratification for your efforts is delayed because the goal is not met until some time in the future.

> *Timing is critical for some goals—as when you hurry to get what you want before someone else does. Other times being first to get something is not best. "The early bird gets the worm, but the second mouse gets the cheese."*

When you want to *have* something, time is money. You exchange your time for money so you can purchase things. Your employer probably pays you for your time by the hour, day, week, or month. You make payments on time; mortgages, credit cards, and rental agreements have due dates that are rigid and unyielding. You pay money for time; lawyers, accountants, plumbers, and telephone companies charge fees by the minute. Time and money are closely related when you want to *have* something.

Time is less of an issue when you set a goal to *be* something. Speed is meaningless when there is no way to measure your progress. *Being* goals have no endpoint or deadline that must be reached by a certain time or date. When you are on the right path and you know that your direction is more important than your destination, time is almost irrelevant. While *being* goals don't allow procrastination, there is no hurry either. A slower pace can be more rewarding than the fast track. The speed at which you travel your path is less important than the enjoyment you experience while on the journey. Without a limitation of time, there is no feeling of failure.

> *"Many people take no care of their money till they come nearly to the end of it, and others do the same with their time."*
> —Johann von Goethe

> *Patience and procrastination can appear as twins, but one is intelligent and the other is lazy.*

SMARTER goals actually do have a deadline. If you personally want to reap the benefits of your goal to *be* something, the only formidable time limitation you have is your lifetime. You must get on the right path before you die. Death is a real *deadline.*

Throughout history people have made great accomplishments that were not recognized until after they died. Herman Melville wrote the classic whale tale *Moby Dick*, but the saga did not become successful until after he died in 1891. Elias Howe invented the sewing machine but died penniless. Artists like Paul Cezanne, Vincent Van Gogh, and Giorgione produced paintings that are now worth millions, but they died in poverty. Perhaps they never enjoyed material wealth, but hopefully they all enjoyed their journeys.

The significance of time in "being" and "having" goals is as different as it is in games of football and baseball

Goals set to *have* something have time limits like those in a professional football game. Time is of the essence in football. The game is played for sixty minutes. When there is action on the field, a clock ticks away, displaying the time remaining in each quarter. There is even a two-minute warning that lets everyone know when the game is almost over. The game ends when the clock runs out of time. The only exception is when the score is tied and a little extra time is added to decide the winner in a sudden-death finish.

Goals set to *be* something are not limited by time, much like a baseball game in which time is not a big issue. A clock does not determine the length of the game. A baseball game is not over until the last batter is out or one team gets more runs than the other in the last inning. Certainly there are events in a baseball game that have time limits (often established by the whim of an umpire) just as there are things that must be done within a set amount of time for all goals. However, the baseball game itself can go on and on and on, just as goals set to *be* something never have to end. Whatever you wish to *be*, there is always room for improvement.

Goal setting and gardening

So often we measure success by what we reap rather than what we sow. If your goal is to *have* things, then the harvest is all that is important. If your goal is to *be* something, then what you are growing is the measure of your success.

Setting a goal to *have* something is like gardening with only the harvest in mind. The thoughts you think are like the seeds you plant in a garden. Some ideas and some seeds take longer than others to germinate, sprout, grow, mature, and create a harvest. Your plans and actions may not produce the end results you expect to see for days or months or even years. Gratification is delayed until you reach your goal to have the thing you want.

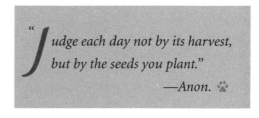

"Judge each day not by its harvest, but by the seeds you plant."
—*Anon.*

If you plant peas you can expect a crop in sixty-five days. Corn that is planted and cultivated will take around one hundred days to mature. Asparagus might need two years to take root, while fruit trees might require many more years before they produce apples, oranges, or cherries. Gratification in gardening is delayed if you measure success by what you harvest.

Setting a goal to *be* something is like gardening for the pure enjoyment of working with seeds and soil and the cultivation of living vegetation. It means having what you want while you are gardening, not just reaping the harvest. Success in the garden does not have to wait until the fall. For many people with green thumbs, a garden is appreciated long before the plants are mature. They realize success through every step of the growing process. They enjoy a feeling of success when the ground is turned over and prepared for planting. They feel success when the seeds are sown, the sprouts break through the dirt, and the plants are firmly established in the soil. They realize success when the plants begin to flower and blossom. Gardens can be very gratifying, even if fruits and vegetables are never harvested.

Thoughts grow into reality. Seeds of thoughts grow into crops of reality. Be aware of what seeds you are planting. You must be able to visualize the end product so that your garden produces the crop you desire. No matter how hard it tries, a lettuce seed will never produce tomatoes. A watermelon seed cannot sprout vines that produce pumpkins. An acorn can only develop into an oak; no one can make it become a spruce. The thoughts you think are the seeds that grow and create your world. What you sow is what you will get.

Delayed gratification

Sometimes we do not pursue goals because we believe they will take too long to accomplish. We scrap many projects because of delays or postponements.

Many of us want results and we want them now. Our lives run on the philosophy of, "Buy now, pay later." We naturally desire instant gratification.

If a healthy nursing puppy is not crying, its stomach is probably full. If the mother leaves the puppy and the puppy gets hungry or cold, the puppy will start to cry. Puppies communicate by whimpering and whining when they want something. As the puppies grow older, whining stops working so they start barking to get what they want. Eventually, the mother dog doesn't listen to the barking and the puppies have to get their own food or go hungry.

People aren't so different from puppies when it comes to whining. Typical youngsters cry to get what they want. If they are hungry and want food, they cry. If they want candy, they cry. If they want attention, they cry. If they want clean clothes, they scream until they get a fresh change. When they are upset, they cry until they are content or just worn out. It doesn't take long for babies to learn that crying usually works to get what they want, but not always.

Children are quick to find other ways to get what they want when whining and crying no longer work. Kids don't bark like puppies, but some throw temper tantrums if their desires are not met. Some get into trouble to draw attention to their needs. Some whine to make situations go the way they want. Loud crying, complaining, and whining usually work to get children what they want, but not always.

As children grow up, they lose the cute control over their parents that they hoped would last a lifetime. They don't always get what they demand and sometimes have to wait a long time for what they want. Worse yet, they learn that some things have to be earned. So they find jobs and become employed. They trade their time for money to buy the things they dream of having. Labor usually works to get what they want, but not always.

Some people just take what they want. If they want food, they take it. If they want money, they steal it. If they want a car, a television, jewelry, or money, they rob a store or a neighbor. Sometimes these people are caught by the authorities and pay for their misdeeds. Stealing usually works to get them what they want, but not always. Somewhere along the way, all crimes create consequences and are punished.

Some of us never change our way of thinking as we grow older. From the time we are little, if we want something that we think will make us happy, we attempt to find a way to get it. Some of us are still pursuing happiness by trying to obtain the things we think will make us happy. And we will use any method imaginable—legal or illegal, moral or immoral, right or wrong—to get what we want. Perhaps you have taken a cookie from a cookie jar or a pencil from a desk at work. Petty pilfering seems trivial, but it is stealing nonetheless. Whether it is candy or a car, getting what we want can seem to make us happy, but the happiness is often fleeting. It is with us only until we want to have something else.

Delayed gratification is not required when your goal is set to *be* something. When you are confidently progressing in the direction of what you want to *be*, you will be continually gratified by your position on the path. If your goal is to be happy, you can fulfill your goal right now by thinking happy thoughts. You don't have to give up your goal to have things, but you might want to give that kind of goal less priority.

> *Learning to invest your time wisely is one of the greatest assets you can acquire to create a successful life. It takes observation and patience. Knowing what you really should be doing with your time—what is urgent, what is important, when to act, when to wait—will be key to your success.*

"I'd give anything to be a vet"

I have lost track of how many times I've heard children say, "I want to be a veterinarian when I grow up." When I ask them why, they usually answer, "Because I like animals." When I ask if there are other reasons, some say they want to *be* a doctor so they can *have* things. They want to have nice houses and cars, work in big clinics, and make lots of money. They have the desire to *be* something, a veterinarian, but their underlying reason for becoming a doctor is to *have* things like money, a house, a nice work environment, or other things money can buy.

Just as often as kids have said they wanted to be a veterinarian, I have heard adults say, "I was going to be a vet but...." Then they list their excuses: "I didn't have good grades in school." "I didn't have the money to pay the tuition." "I didn't want to go to college for eight years." "The college was too far from home." "I had to do something else." "I got married."

I smile when I hear that statement, "I'd give anything to be a vet." My response is always the same. I don't say it out loud, but I think to myself, "No, you wouldn't." If people would give anything, they would invest the countless hours of reading, studying, observing, and interacting with animals and teachers required to *be* a veterinarian. Many people might like to *have* a college degree in veterinary medicine, but they don't really want to do the things necessary to *be* an animal doctor. They want to be a vet, but they lack the desire to *be* a student, to *be* self-motivated, to *be* dedicated, and to *be* relentless in the pursuit of their goal. With a few exceptions, people who would truly give anything to fulfill their dreams could do so just like anyone else.

It takes about eight years of college to *have* a veterinary degree. For most graduates, it takes a lifetime of commitment to *be* a veterinarian. The goal to *have* a college diploma may have a schedule and a deadline, but the goal to *be* a veterinarian has only a beginning. There is not always a point at which one can say, "I am now a veterinarian." Officially, that happens at graduation from veterinary school, but in reality, it happens to some students well before graduation. Some of us were veterinarians even before we started college. Of course we had a lot to learn and we could not practice for pay, but we thought and talked and acted as if we were doctors even in our undergraduate years.

Some of my college classmates graduated from veterinary college and never really became what we traditionally think of as a veterinarian. They went to work in a laboratory or industry or business. Some never used their degrees to help animals directly although they have been beneficial to society without practicing veterinary medicine or surgery. The point is this: there is a difference between *having* a diploma from a veterinary college and *being* a veterinarian. One takes time and money. It is a goal that can be reached in a limited amount of time. The other requires commitment and dedication beyond the books and lectures and classrooms. The goal to *be* a veterinarian is ongoing and endless. It is timeless.

Will you find the time to think about the ideas in this book? Will you take the time to plan your future? Maybe you will never *find* the time. You must *make* the time. *Take* the time now to establish your goals. Now is the time to decide what you want to *be*. Once you know what and who you want to *be*, you can begin your endless journey.

> *As long as you are certain you are proceeding in the right direction—as long as your life is on course— every minute of your time is invested as it should be.*

Those who are truly successful know that SMARTER goals are timeless.

Emotionally stabilizing

Somewhere along the way, we need to realize that *SMARTER Success* can be achieved by setting goals that are emotionally stabilizing.

Normal, healthy emotions vary with your moods and the cycles of hormones in your body. Emotions come and go with the seasons of the year. They fluctuate during various periods of the day. They wax and wane with the pressures you experience in relationships and working environments. And emotions can be dependent upon what you eat or what is eating you.

Emotional stability means:

…controlling emotions.

…avoiding extreme mood swings.

…keeping emotional fluctuation within a reasonable range.

…alleviating depression.

…maintaining a happy disposition most of the time.

When a goal is set to *have* something, emotions encourage you to compete for your goal. The desire to acquire can elicit extreme emotions, both positive and negative. Competition can invoke very strong feelings that motivate athletes to perform better, employees to work more efficiently, and individuals to improve their performance in any area of life. Failure to achieve a goal in competition can result in sadness and depression.

Competition for the things you want can elicit envy, selfishness, animosity, and strife. Rivalry for power can bring out contention, resentment, spite, and jealousy. The desire to have more than you need can lead to greed, piggishness, and indignation. The emotions that are good for getting what you want to *have* can get out of control and produce problems no one would ever desire.

In the diagrams that follow, the solid wavy line plots the variations of emotions as they change over time. The shape and location of this line are the most important features of the graphs.

The vertical line or Y-axis is a measure of happiness and sadness. Halfway up the vertical line is a point of neutrality. The horizontal dotted line that starts at this point marks a state of emotionless tranquility. Points above the dotted line register increases in happiness. Points below the dotted line register increases in sadness. The lowest end of the vertical line represents severe depression; the top represents manic euphoria.

The bottom horizontal line depicts a scale of time. Divisions along the horizontal X-axis represent units of time: minutes, hours, days, seasons, or years. Each mark on the time line might denote minutes if you were measuring emotions during a football game. Each point could represent hours if you were plotting emotions throughout a normal day. They might indicate months if you were examining emotions as they rise and fall during different seasons of the year.

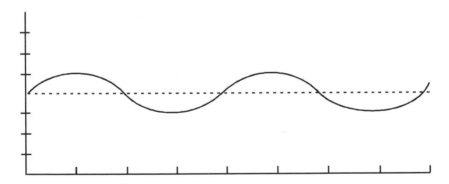

With appropriate labels on the lines in the diagram above, the wavy line could be a recording of the normal variations of your emotions during a day.

You wake up neutral, become happy you are alive, and the line goes up. Then you realize you have to go to work and the line heads down. The traffic during your trip to work makes you a little tense, you become unhappy, and the solid line dips below the dotted line. When you arrive at your place of employment, you greet colleagues, share a few stories, and the line goes up indicating you are becoming happier. You continue to improve and your emotional state climbs above the dotted line until the boss tells you to get to work and the line heads down again. The events of the day worsen and improve, influencing your emotions. The line goes up and down throughout the day but never sways too far from neutrality.

Diurnal variation is the term scientists use to describe changes we all experience through the course of a day. It's normal to cycle from being happy to being melancholy, and from being sad to being glad again, over and over throughout the day, week, month, or year. As long as you don't get too sad or too mad or too angry or even too happy, your life proceeds smoothly.

Trouble begins to occur when emotions get out of control. The extremes of emotions are displayed when people have large mood swings. They become extremely happy and then extremely sad. Severe sadness or over-excited euphoria can lead to activities that are unhealthy and dangerous. People who act this way for no obvious reason have a condition referred to as manic-depressive disorder.

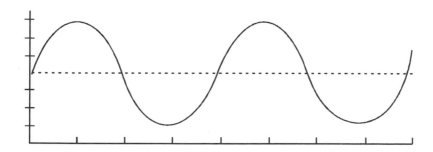

The diagram above depicts the mood swings of a person who is out of control. There are short times when the person is neutral or in the middle area of the graph, but much of the time the person is extremely happy or very sad. If the time line indicates minutes, this person could have a serious mental illness, being happy one minute and sad the next. The mood swings might be spread out over a longer period of time, which could be more manageable, but it would still be difficult to function and interact with other people when in the extreme areas.

> *Perhaps you have seen a man who has profound and sudden emotional mood swings. He may walk back and forth screaming at the top of his lungs, then suddenly sit in a chair, put his face in his hands, and weep uncontrollably. Even though these extreme swings of happiness and sadness might be repeated several times in a single evening, they are not always the signs and symptoms of mental disease. These activities are seen as normal behavior when exhibited by basketball coaches during close games.*

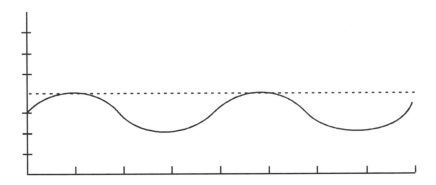

Some people have ups and downs during the day, but are never really happy. The plotting of their emotions produces a solid line that never rises above neutral. They experience little if any enjoyment in life. They seem to be sad all the time. They frown more than they smile. Life is not much fun when all of your thoughts and emotions are sad or at best neutral.

For some people the line hardly curves and is charted even lower. If the graph of a person's life is fairly straight and at the bottom of the graph, that individual is experiencing chronic depression.

A happy graph

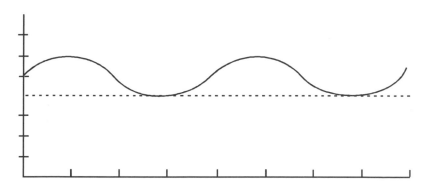

Variation in your emotional states is normal and important as it is just about impossible be happy all the time. Some moments, hours, and days are bound to be happier than others. But it is possible to function above the dotted line most of the time. If the wavy line that describes your feelings looks like the one on the graph above, the worst emotions you feel are neutral. It takes a special attitude to maintain such a level on this chart, but it can be done. Setting a goal to *be* something can help.

The kind of goal you set has a significant influence on your ability to stabilize your emotions. Setting a goal to *be* something can help you maintain a happy attitude and keep the plot of your emotions in the top half of the graph. You actually can set a goal to keep yourself happy. Emotions like anger, hatred, blaming, jealousy, greed, and indignation can be reduced and eventually eliminated by one positive emotion. You may still have the emotions of both sadness and happiness, but the extremes of sorrow and euphoria can be avoided. It may sound simplistic, idealistic, and overly romantic, but all negative emotions can be replaced by one positive emotion: love.

You can create emotional stability by working toward a goal to *be* something. Emotional stability defuses hot issues and prevents manic-depressive situations. You don't need to get all bent out of shape when things don't go your way.

Simple emotions are a natural part of animal lives

Does a deer become frightened while standing by the road at night when it sees headlights of an approaching car? Does a squirrel get excited when it rustles through dead oak leaves and finds an acorn? Does a field mouse fear a red fox who is lurking in the bushes looking for a snack? Does a dog get angry when you take away its bone? Does a cat seek revenge when a human offends it? Does a cow experience love while licking its newborn calf? Do animals really experience emotions?

Of course! Most all animals experience something like our human emotions of happiness, sadness, anger, and fear. Emotions are natural and make life interesting—sometimes enjoyable and sometimes painful.

Manic-depressive disorders seldom occur in the animal world. Animals can have strong emotions, but there is usually a physical reason, such as a life-or-death situation. Humans don't need real reasons to change moods. We can think up irrational, unrealistic, unreasonable, irresponsible reasons for emotions. When our thinking gets out of hand, emotions can run wild. We don't need physical reasons when we can create our own imaginary mental reasons for emotions.

Making unemotional decisions

One of the stronger emotions that people typically display is love for a mate. The emotions that keep two people together in a marriage are some of the most powerful we will ever enjoy. Unfortunately, those emotional bonds can dissipate with time. The positive emotions that first attracted the husband and wife to each other occasionally reverse, become negative, and force them apart. If a marriage ends in divorce, the strong emotions that initially kept two people together can backfire. Negative emotions during a divorce are displayed in feelings of revenge and hatred, as well as offensive behavior including physical violence.

When my first wife filed for divorce, my life was filled with emotions, which at the time were mostly negative. Negative thoughts clouded my thinking and made it difficult for me to make decisions, and many needed to be made. I had many questions about divorce that required answers. I needed to know how to handle the children, lawyers, bills, property division, relatives, friends, and clients. I needed help finding the answers, so I sought counseling from a trusted social worker, Frank Scannell, Ph.D., ACSW.

The counselor never answered a single one of my questions. He never told me what to do, what was right, or what was wrong. Yet every time we met, I left his office knowing the answers to my questions. It was amazing. Somehow he always let me answer my own questions. He helped me to think clearly. And when I could do that, I knew I could make the right (or at least best) decision at the time.

I learned that by controlling my own thoughts I could control my emotions. I had to stop and think about what I was doing. Whenever I had to make a choice, I needed to hesitate, use my intellect, and concentrate on what was right. I needed to refrain from making snap decisions and reacting by how I felt. I had to behave as though my children were watching me, because they were. I had to do my thinking with my head and not with my heart or any other part of my anatomy.

I learned that a good, sound marriage was better than divorce or bachelorhood for my own health and happiness as well as for everyone involved, but this marriage situation was beyond my control. I learned that divorce could be bad for children. It could produce of all kinds of negative behaviors, including psychological problems, under-education, juvenile delinquency, and even suicide. Statistics lead us to believe that divorce increases the chances of everything from bad breath to being hit by a truck, but most children of divorce won't be hit by a truck. The majority usually turn out okay, without serious problems.

I realized that my children would be influenced more by my actions than by the divorce itself. I couldn't keep the family together, but I could continue to give the children what I believe every parent owes their kids: *modeling*. The children would pay more attention to my response to what was happening than they would to what was actually happening. And I may not have been able to con-

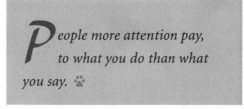

People more attention pay, to what you do than what you say.

trol what happened around me, or what happened to me, but I could control what happened *in* me, in my thoughts and in my actions. I could control how I reacted and responded to emotional situations. I attempted to model self-control for my children. I set a goal to go through the divorce process with emotional stability.

The Four R's:
Realistic—Rational—Responsible—Reasonable

Through my social worker's counseling, I learned about "The Four R's." When emotions are running your life, or when emotions are *ruining* your life, stop. Before you make any significant decision that might be based on emotions, ask yourself four questions that begin with the letter "R":

- **Realistic**—Is the solution to the problem realistic? Is it within the realm of normal expectation?
- **Rational**—Would a sane person make this decision in this way? Does it make sense logically?
- **Responsible**—Is the solution one for which you would want to take credit after it is made? Is it your own decision or are you reacting like a marionette puppet—letting someone else pull your strings? (Wayne Dyer's book, *Pulling Your Own Strings,* can help if you feel someone is yanking your chain and you want to take back control of your life.)
- **Reasonable**—Is the solution within the boundaries of normal common sense? Is it in accordance with sound thinking? Is it fair and not extreme?

Try to use the four "R's" whenever a decision should *not* be made based solely on emotions. By asking if the answer you have decided upon is rational, realistic, reasonable, and responsible, you can be somewhat assured that your decision is not based on emotions alone. The four "R's" promote emotional stability and enhance the chance that you can live with the choices you make.

There is a down side to making decisions in this manner. If you make all of your decisions using the four "R's," you might remove all of the excitement and variety from your life. Living without emotions might mean that your life would always be plotted on the neutral dotted lines in the graphs—never happy, never sad. You would never do anything spontaneously. You would never make capricious choices. You would never make decisions based on intuition. Life without emotions would be boring and monotonous.

Imagine falling in love while making decisions using the four "R's." It is almost impossible because falling in love with another individual is often:

- **Unrealistic**—Most marriages (which are supposed to be very committed relationships of love) end in divorce. To say the feelings you have while courting will never change is to say that you will beat the odds.

Some marriages result in eternal bliss for the couple, but they are rare. Most couples make vows that far exceed what will really be possible.

- **Irrational**—Love doesn't always make sense. Mr. Spock from the television series Star Trek and others from the planet Vulcan have a hard time understanding love. It is illogical. People are not creatures of logic. People are bristling with desires and prejudices, vanity and pride, and emotions that are irrational.
- **Irresponsible**—A new love relationship often means spending time away from old friends and even family. You might cut out from work early or arrive late because of your love affair. A new love makes it hard to concentrate on projects and assignments.
- **Unreasonable**—Why would anyone spend two months' wages on a pretty stone in a fancy ring and then give it away? It's not reasonable. Why do people cry at weddings, which are supposed to be happy events? It's not reasonable.

Without emotions, sporting events like basketball, football, and auto racing would be as exciting as watching paint dry. Without emotions, no one would weep at wakes. People wouldn't get mad when they were betrayed or cheated. There would be no reason to smile or frown. No one would scream when startled or tremble when scared. If we were never glad, sad, mad, or scared, life would be humdrum and uninteresting.

If you want to witness a life without emotions, visit a nursing home or an institution for the mentally challenged. There, due to age, disease, or chemical imbalances in the brain, many of the residents are passionless. Observing how they live their lives can help you appreciate your own life as well as the emotions you experience.

You need to feel emotions to live a satisfying life. Passion puts purpose into your being. Emotions give you the drive and desire to reach goals and accomplish dreams. Living a life without emotions would be like baking a traditional birthday cake without flour and frosting and candles. It can be done, but why? The result would be pitiful. Without texture and taste, a cake would not be worth making. Without feelings and emotions, life would not be worth living.

Material success is worthless without mental success

It doesn't matter how successful the rest of the world thinks you are. What matters is how successful *you* think you are. If you do not believe you are successful, nothing anyone in the world can say or do will make a difference until you change your mind. You will be successful only to the degree you think you are successful.

Examples abound of people who appear to be successful but apparently don't feel successful. You can pick up any popular newspaper or magazine and read of successful, rich, and famous celebrities who are depressed, using drugs, abusing power, or have even committed suicide. Countless others who you would think are successful do the same. Because they don't feel successful, they cannot be happy. Because they are not happy, they turn to alcohol and chemicals that alter their thinking or end their lives.

The story of Wallace Carothers, a name you might not recognize, illustrates the point that seemingly successful people don't always feel successful. Wallace was born in a mid-western town in Iowa in 1896. The son of a teacher, he was the oldest of four children. Wallace loved to read English literature, stories by Mark Twain, and books about the life of Thomas Edison. He loved classical music, art, sports, and politics. Although Wallace came from a family of Scotch-Irish farmers and artisans, he was destined to be the family's first scientist.

Carothers studied science and accounting in college. He received a master's degree and held several teaching positions in universities where he began his research in organic chemistry. Carothers appeared to enjoy research more than teaching and was especially interested in how individual elements were held together in complex molecules. At Harvard, he started experimenting with very large molecules (macromolecules), polymers with very high molecular weights.

When a laboratory of the DuPont Company in Wilmington, Delaware, offered Wallace a position in which he could continue his research, he accepted with delight. Although he did not have teaching responsibilities, he took on huge responsibilities managing a division of the laboratory. Wallace was good with people and worked with enthusiasm and creativity.

His dedication to research inspired devotion and admiration in the people who worked with him. He was recognized for making some of the most highly valued and notable accomplishments of his time. His research and developments were so significant that they continue to affect our lives even today.

Here is an example. Due to political and trade troubles with Japan during the years before World War II, silk was becoming harder and more expensive to obtain. DuPont wanted to develop a synthetic fiber to replace silk. Carothers and his associates took on the task, and in 1934 they pulled out of a test tube their first long, strong, flexible strands of a synthetic polymer fiber. The corporation patented their discovery as "nylon". In the course of his research, Carothers published thirty-one papers, establishing general theories about polymers and standardizing the terminology of the field. He had brought the world not just nylon, but knowledge of natural polymers and how they are formed.

> *Nylon was first used for fishing line, surgical sutures, and toothbrush bristles. The new fiber was "as strong as steel, as fine as a spider's web." Nylon and nylon stockings were introduced to the American public at the New York World's Fair in 1939. In fact, the "ny" in nylon comes from the initials of New York.*

Carothers' reputation grew. Though rather shy of publicity, he wrote papers and gave speeches, and was the first organic chemist elected to the National Academy of Sciences. But while he was becoming rich and famous, he struggled with depression. He became obsessed with the thought that his life's work was meaningless, and suffered mounting manic-depressive mood swings.

In 1936 he married Helen Sweetman, who also worked at DuPont. They had a daughter, whom Carothers was never to know. Early in 1937 his favorite sister died suddenly. That loss added to his depression, and in April of that year he committed suicide by consuming a small dose of cyanide, a powerful poison he had carried in his pocket for years.

How could this brilliant man contribute so much to science and humanity and yet be so unhappy? Perhaps he was driven by goals to *have* more rather than to *be* more. He had talent, intelligence, a wonderful career, a loving wife, many friends and followers, but he wasn't happy. He had fame, fortune, and a family, but was not satisfied with his accomplishments. Perhaps SMARTER goals could have helped him be happy. Perhaps SMARTER goals could have given him a purpose in life and helped him stabilize his mood swings. Striving for SMARTER goals might have motivated him to live longer, to know his daughter, and to contribute even more to the world.

The world needs scientists, inventors, physicians, and entertainers who focus their energies and enthusiasm on specific targets, set ambitious goals, and then attain them. Those individuals can do even more for society and themselves if they are happy and maintain emotional stability.

The depression Carothers suffered was in part the result of thinking depressing thoughts. The pain and suffering people with emotional diseases bring upon themselves are no less real than those caused by viruses and germs. Consistently thinking depressing thoughts can alter your body so much that chemical imbalances occur which need medical attention. If you become so depressed you can't think straight, see a qualified health-care professional for help. If you think you can improve your life by yourself, consider setting a goal to think happy thoughts always.

Post-accomplishment depression

When a woman gives birth to a healthy child, she has fulfilled one of the most significant goals in nature—reproduction is necessary to prevent extinction of a species. The goal to *have* a baby has been accomplished. The goal to *be* a parent has just begun. The days that follow the arrival of a child should be the happiest time in a parent's life, yet some mothers become sad and despondent. They have reached a goal to *have* a baby but are not happy to *be* a parent. Their spirits can get so low that they have a condition called postpartum depression. This serious condition is caused by many factors and can range from mild to life-threatening.

Similar depression can occur to anyone after any major event, especially during holiday seasons. We buy presents and make elaborate plans for family dinners and parties, then become exhausted and even sad when the festivities are over. We get so busy planning to be happy that we don't take time just to be happy. People can get so sad that they have a condition called postholiday depression.

When a goal to *have* something is achieved, there is usually a phase of jubilation, but emotional highs can sag to emotional lows very quickly. Depression can easily occur following a graduation, marriage, job promotion, or any other significant goal. One reason for this post-accomplishment depression is the lack of a new goal. Because there is no longer a goal in sight, there is nothing to work toward. Without a goal to *have* something new, there is no emotional drive to give spark to life.

The time in between goals can be dangerous if you are the kind of person who always sets goals to *have* things. You have to imagine new dreams, set new challenges, and establish new goals or you may face depression. If you become depressed, a new goal might bring you out of it. When you reach that goal, you will once again feel the high that is realized when your goal to have something is met. The highs and lows involved with obtaining things or attaining success can lead to emotional <u>in</u>stability.

Setting a goal to *be* something can help you avoid depression. Emotional stability can free you of symptoms of headaches and muscle pains produced by tension. Emotional stability allows you to function when the going gets really rough. It allows you to be flexible. Because *being* goals don't have an end, there is no post-accomplishment depression.

Emotional stability reduces the anxiety that comes with high expectations. When you realize that every action you take is part of the process of becoming what you desire, you never expect to be perfect, only better than you were before.

When a person earns a professional degree from a veterinary college, passes examinations, and obtains a license, the individual can then practice veterinary medicine and surgery. The same is true for physicians and other professionals. No one earns a license to *do* medicine. Whether the doctor is a veterinarian who works on your pets or a physician who works on your body, doctors are just practicing medicine. Likewise, whatever you dream of *being*, you must realize that you will always have the possibility of being better. Practice will never make you perfect. At best, practice will help you improve. The great motivational speaker Les Brown taught me that and I'll never forget it.

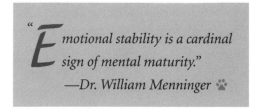

"*E motional stability is a cardinal sign of mental maturity.*"
—*Dr. William Menninger*

Maintaining emotional stability

How do you maintain emotional stability? How can you prevent getting depressed? How can you avoid letting joy overwhelm you? Counseling and medication can help, but if you want to do something for yourself, consider these twelve factors that help create emotional stability in your life:

1. Live in the present, moment by moment.
2. Control what you can; stop wasting time trying to change what you can't.
3. Cooperate and harmonize with life.
4. Avoid self-pity.
5. Cultivate the virtues of love, integrity, honor, and loyalty.
6. Participate in some form of voluntary activity to supplement your required daily work.
7. Eliminate suspicion and resentment.
8. Redirect any natural hostile tendency into creative and constructive energy; use competitive games to provide social outlets for aggressive emotions.
9. Realize that although you are a part of something much bigger than you can comprehend, you can still make a difference regardless of your size, shape, education, or intelligence.
10. Talk out problems with trusted friends or professionals. The very act of telling your stories to sympathetic listeners is one of the most powerful therapeutic tools in medicine.
11. Detach yourself from the outcome of events that won't affect you.
12. Set goals to *be* something rather than to *have* something.

Getting beyond the need to prove you are right

Emotional stability is strengthened when you can feel that your own ideas are correct, without feeling the need to prove someone else wrong. Families have broken up due to religious conflicts. Countries have gone to war over political differences. Seldom does anyone win a debate regarding religion or politics. Arguing is often pointless because these subjects are based mostly on faith and opinions. When opinions differ, harmonious discussions are rare. Even if the other side quits arguing, that doesn't mean you have won the debate. There is an adage, "People convinced against their will are of the same opinion still." Because you see things from a different perspective, you form different opinions and beliefs and therefore have a different faith. That's normal.

If you can accept that all people are different and have different beliefs—no two people can have exactly the same religious beliefs or political views—then you can be content with your own faith and feel no incentive to force your ideas onto others. You can listen to other people present their views of life and how things work. You can discuss religion and refuse to argue issues. You can talk about politics and avoid heated debates. Differences in opinions are natural. It's just a matter of perspective. You may not agree with others, but you don't have to prove them right or wrong, especially when proof is impossible. Some things transcend the need for proof and can be accepted simply on faith.

Seeing is believing; observing is knowing

Things are not always as they might at first appear. Seeing is one thing. Observing is another. Observation involves using not only your eyes but also your mind to compile and comprehend what you see. Observation involves seeing details and relating those details to what you have seen and experienced before.

Fans of English detective stories are quite familiar with the expression, "Elementary, my dear Watson." The line was made famous by the stories of Sherlock Holmes, the detective hero in the tales by Sir Arthur Conan Doyle. Dr. Watson, Sherlock's sidekick, often asked Holmes how he had solved a case that baffled Watson and the rest of Scotland Yard. Most who were reading or listening to the stories couldn't figure them out either. Holmes would explain the solution to the mystery, making it sound so simple and obvious that Watson would respond with, "But see here, Holmes, I saw the very same thing you did."

To which Holmes would reply, "Ah, yes, my dear Dr. Watson, but you did not observe what I observed!"

Holmes and Watson saw the same crime scenes and clues, but Holmes observed more closely, from a different perspective, and therefore perceived things differently. We all see things from different perspectives. That is why we have different opinions, beliefs, and religions. We observe details and relationships between objects and events to greater or lesser extents. Therefore, we each develop a different point of view.

Emotional stability in life is really quite elementary. When you respect the fact that others see things differently, you can observe without passing judgment. Most of the time you can stabilize your emotions by choosing to be happy rather than thinking you need to be right. You don't need to prove that your thoughts are correct, as long as your thoughts produce peace.

> "*S*hedding a backpack filled with hatred, blame, anger, and guilt makes your journey through life a whole lot easier."
>
> —Vetdini ❧

You have the right to be angry or jealous, to feel guilty, and to hate. You have the right to be sad and sick. But why would you want to, when you can choose to be happy and healthy? The choice begins with choosing your thoughts and then setting your goals. Accepting responsibility for your own thoughts and decisions is a major step toward maintaining emotional stability. When you know you are on the right path to *be* something, you will still experience variations in your emotions, but you will avoid extreme emotional highs and lows and maintain balanced mental health.

If you ever get depressed or angry that things aren't going your way, stop and ask yourself a question that is short and snappy. "Would I rather be right, or would I rather be happy?" Do yourself and everyone around you a favor by choosing to be happy.

Those who are truly successful know that SMARTER goals are emotionally stabilizing.

Relationship building

Somewhere along the way, we need to realize that *SMARTER Success* can be achieved by setting goals that are relationship building.

*T*his chapter describes the last and perhaps most important of the seven characteristics of a SMARTER goal. When you set a goal to *be* something, you are attempting to make a positive influence on your future. Because you can control only your own thoughts and actions, the goals you set are for you personally. Even though they are not intended to control others, your goals can affect everyone around you. Therefore, you must consider the goals and desires of others when you make your plans.

> *"No goal is worthy of pursuit if you cannot share it with someone along the way."*
>
> —*Vetdini* ❧

We need relationships not only to be happy and successful, but also simply to exist—no one can survive completely alone. *No man is an island.* Some people are peninsulas and do well without being well-connected to the rest of the world, but we all need

❧ "A friend is someone you can do nothing with, and enjoy it."

—*The Optimist*

other people at some time. Perhaps you would like to have a lot of money rather than many friends. Perhaps you have had bad relationships with people and would rather live in isolation. Even if you prefer to have a dog as your best friend rather than a person, you need to have relationships to function as a human being.

Abraham Maslow's research into the needs of humans showed that belongingness and love were desired almost as much as food, shelter, and security. We want to be part of a family. We want to belong to a community. We want to love and be loved. And what is love if there is no one to share it? We need other people in our lives. We need relationships, companionships, and friendships.

> "*Of all the things which wisdom provides to make life entirely happy, much the greatest is the possession of friendship.*"
>
> —*Epicurus* 🐾

Imagine you have made it to the top. You have it all. Think what it would be like to accomplish every goal you ever set. Give it some thought. Imagine for a moment that you are a complete success, by any measure you choose to use. However you define success, you have made it to the top.

Now, imagine looking back at your life when it is coming to an end. How did you accomplish your goals? What were the most significant factors that aided your accomplishments? What events were crucial to your advancement? Did anyone help you along the way? Did you have a mentor who inspired you? What would you miss most about your journey to the top? What memories would you highly cherish about your path to success? What recollections would be the most important?

One way to learn what it is like to reflect on a long, successful life is to talk with people who have previously tread the path to prosperity. To find out what people might expect to look back upon when they got to the top, I interviewed people who had "been there and done that." I talked with hundreds of

🐾 "Don't worry about who doesn't like you, who has more, or who's doing what. Instead, let's cherish the relationships we have with those who DO love us."

—Erma Bombeck

successful retired people about their experiences in school, business, home-making, and parenting. We discussed what it was like to have lived a long and successful life.

The fascinating elderly people I interviewed all told me the same basic things. What they remembered most fondly and missed the most were the relationships— the interactions with other people. They treasured their families and friends more than possessions. They missed their classmates from high school and their playmates from summers

> "*There is nothing on this earth more to be prized than true friendship.*"
> —*St. Thomas Aquinas* ❧

long ago. They revered the bonds they shared with old business associates, employers, and fellow employees. They missed meeting with their old colleagues, customers, and even their competitors. The relationships that were developed along the way were the most valuable rewards from their life's work.

Many of the older people with whom I talked had been financially successful and relatively wealthy at one time. Others had very few possessions and lived in small rooms at nursing homes. Never did I hear a person over seventy tell me that money, houses, jewelry, and other tangible possessions were more important than relationships. No matter what material wealth they had accumulated, they felt relationships with family members and friends were more important than anything else in their lives.

> "*It is great to have friends when one is young, but indeed it is still more so when you are getting old. When we are young, friends are, like everything else, a matter of course. In the old days we know what it means to have them.*"
> —*Edvard Grieg* ❧

❧ "The language of friendship is not words but meanings."
—Henry David Thoreau

> *Our elders say success in life is about relationships; yet younger people still measure success by what they can accumulate and control. Certainly priorities change with age, but if you know that relationships will someday be your most valued possession, perhaps you will do more to nurture them now.*

Are relationships assets?

Perhaps your goal has always been to acquire things. Perhaps you dream of attaining power or prestige. Perhaps you are working to create a great investment portfolio that will ensure endless income. Perhaps you are saving money because you were told you should. Money is important and the more money you have the more important you will be. Right?

I have never filled out an application for a mortgage or a credit card that had spaces to list my friends and how much I valued them. Never has a banker asked for the names of my closest companions on a financial statement. My accountant never asks for a reconciliation of relationships on my year-end profit and loss statement. The Internal Revenue Service does not tax friendships…yet.

Bankers and accountants deal with money and therefore with the value of tangible things. Friendships and relationships are abstract and not as easy to measure; yet they are much more valuable. The financial institutions and the government can determine the value of your money and your property. But to know what your life is really worth, you must count your friends. Anyone can make money. It takes a special person to make a friend, to be a friend.

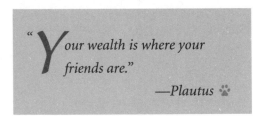

"*Your wealth is where your friends are.*"

—*Plautus*

The value of stocks and bonds on Wall Street is measured in money. When we take stock of the bonds we create with people, they are immeasurable.

"A man cannot be said to succeed in this life who does not satisfy one friend."
—Henry David Thoreau

To have a friend, be a friend

Happiness comes from good relationships. If the goals you work for will build relationships, then they are certain to bring you happiness. On the other hand, if you crush people, step on toes, and walk all over others, you may get to the top, but it might be very costly in terms of friendships. You must make sure the goals you set for yourself will not interfere with present, precious friendships. You need to create goals that will not only preserve old relationships but also develop new ones.

Perhaps you could set a goal to *have* a friend and use the old SMART system to get one. You might be very specific about the person you want to have as a friend. Every day you could do something in a measurable way to develop the friendship. The things you do could be acceptable and realistic and you could set a time by which you would make a person your friend. But manipulating and scheming

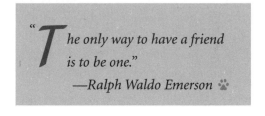

"*The only way to have a friend is to be one.*"
—*Ralph Waldo Emerson*

will not build a solid relationship. You can do nice things for people that are specific, measurable, acceptable, realistic and limited by time, but nothing you do can *force* another person to like you. To *have* a friend, the other person must want to *be* your friend.

The wisdom of Emerson is fundamental to *SMARTER Success*. If you want to *have* a friend, you must first *be* a friend. Although you can't coerce a person be your friend, you can do things to influence how people relate to you. You can't control the feelings and emotions of other people, but you can attempt to control your own actions and try to *be* friendly.

Relationships take effort and energy if they are to develop into strong friendships. Somewhere along the way, someone told me, "You can make more friends in a couple of months by becoming interested in other people than you can in a decade by trying to get people interested in you." I have found that to be true.

"It is not so much your friends' help that helps you, as the confidence of their help."
—Epicurus

> *You might try the following in a conversation with a new acquaintance. Whatever the other person says, respond with a similar comment or question about the person speaking. If asked what your occupation is, give a simple answer and ask what the other person does. Follow that with an open-ended question about that particular line of work. Focus the conversation on the other person and see if it doesn't make a big difference in your relationship.*

Setting goals to *be* something rather than to *have* something can encourage friendships and win-win relationships. When you understand and fully realize the importance of relationships, you can learn more about getting along with people, partnering, parenting, and relationships. Books from the self-help section of bookstores and libraries contain a plethora of ideas you can put to work immediately to build relationships. Dale Carnegie's best-selling book, *How to Win Friends and Influence People,* is a good book with which to start.

Here are just a few quick tips on how you can create better relationships.

1. Acknowledge the presence of others.

Say, "Hi" to everyone you meet. At least give them a smile. Make eye contact with people. Continue to communicate to the degree you wish to develop the relationship.

2. Let others know you care about them.

Everyone has a craving for appreciation at some time in life. Lack of appreciation is a major factor that contributes to poor job performance and low employee morale. It also is one reason why wives abandon families, fathers desert their children, and children run away from home. Attention deficits displayed by children often start with attention deficits from parents.

> "*Wear a smile and have friends; wear a scowl and have wrinkles.*"
>
> —George Eliot ❖

❖ "Create friendships not for comfort and compassion when you need sympathy, but rather for hope and strength when you need encouragement."

—Anon.

Appreciate your relationships and maintain an attitude of gratitude for your friends. Friendships are made stronger if you promote and protect each other's health and happiness. The greatest gift you can give your child, your spouse, or your friend is attention. Every relationship can benefit from focused attention.

> *"The desire for the feeling of importance is one of the chief distinguishing differences between mankind and the animals."*
>
> —Dale Carnegie

3. Learn what others want.

"Do unto others as you would have others do unto you" is the Golden Rule. One better is, "Do unto others as they would want you to do unto them." Neither rule is easy to follow and the second one is impossible until you learn how other people want to be treated. You can do that by asking them or by trying to look at situations from their perspective. When you supply others with their needs and desires, you naturally build strong relationships.

By learning what animals want, we can develop relationships with them that provide us with what we want. Food usually works as an incentive to teach a dog a new trick, to get a bird to sit on your finger, or to have a horse come when you whistle. Offering animals something they want works to create the response you desire and also build a relationship.

A newborn calf can walk within minutes of birth, but it would rather just stand and suck milk from its mother. When it is time to move the calf into a pen or a barn, it can be a real chore to push or lead a ninety-pound animal where it doesn't want to go. Rather than struggling with the calf to make it do what it would rather not, smarter farmers let the calf suck on a couple of their fingers. The calf thinks it will eventually get the milk it wants. The farmer slowly and gently moves toward the barn pen, and the calf walks along sucking as it goes. By discovering

"Be slow in choosing a friend, slower in changing."

—Benjamin Franklin

what the calf wants, farmers get what they want and the task of moving the calf becomes easy.

With animals or with people, if you can determine the desires of others and satisfy them, you will create countless opportunities for friendships.

4. Be polite.

Don't hold back on compliments. Use kind words including "Please" and "Thank you." Reinforce appropriate actions with words of encouragement.

5. Be honest.

Your integrity should be one of your most prized virtues. When your goal is to *be* something, dishonesty hurts you more than anything. If you lie to your child when your goal is to be a parent, you fail to be a respectable parent. If you cheat on your spouse when your goal is to be a desirable spouse, you fail to be an admirable spouse. If you swindle a friend when your goal is to be a friend, you fail to be one. When you act counter to your spiritual beliefs, you deceive no one but yourself. Goals that involve being a spouse, parent, friend, or simply a good person demand honesty. Relationships are apt to last a lifetime when they are built on a foundation of truth and sincerity.

When you set a goal to *have* something, you will be tempted to get what you want in less than honest ways. If your goal is to have money, you might find it convenient to hide funds from your spouse, pilfer a child's savings, borrow permanently from a friend, or embezzle from an employer. If your goal is to have other things, you may be attracted by the idea that you can have them before you earn them. Shoplifting, robbery, and theft are all forms of stealing that will enable you to have what you want, but none is an honest activity. Such crimes won't help when you set your goal with the SMARTER technique. You can't steal what you want to *be*!

❧ "Friendship that flames goes out in a flash."

—Thomas Fuller

6. Avoid relationship killers.

True friendships never end, according to the sage who said, "He who ceases to be a friend never was one." However, there are many factors that can sever and destroy even the best of friendships.

Setting a goal to *have* a thing means competing with others for money or power. Competition for things that are in limited supply can produce winners and losers. With few exceptions, other people now control the material things you want to obtain. If you wish to obtain things from others, you need to establish some kind of relationship with them. The relationship will influence how and when you get what you desire. If you steal what you want, a bad relationship is sure to follow the conviction of the crime. If you purchase the article in a fair trade, you will strengthen the relationship. If two friends are selling the same type of product, purchasing from one may alienate the other. If either the seller or the buyer feels cheated, the relationship will suffer.

Distances and differences can affect relationships. If you have a goal to move to a bigger house, you may have to move to a different neighborhood. That may mean losing touch with old friends, a price you must be prepared to pay in addition to realty costs. Friendships change as financial situations change. Lottery winners make new friends but lose precious old ones. A promotion, a new job, an increase in pay, or a major inheritance can separate you from your former peers. And friendships in political races are tested whether friends are running for the same office or voting for opposing parties.

Business relationships

When I graduated from veterinary school and established my own general practice, I had no clients. None! No one really knew me in the little town where I started my practice. The widow of the veterinarian who previously practiced in the area introduced me to a few farmers. Eventually I met new

"For what is your friend that you should seek him with hours to kill? Seek him always with hours to live."

—Kahlil Gibran

clients by referrals and at the bank and the grocery store. But I needed to let more people know I was in business to help with their pets and cattle.

A veterinary clinic is like any other business in that it must have sales to generate income. Right out of school, I had no training in the science and art of selling. I had spent years studying to help animals remain healthy, but I never had any training in business marketing or sales. Several advertising agencies wanted to help solve my problem. The local printer wanted me to buy ad space in the newspaper. The telephone Yellow Pages people wanted me to place a big ad in the phone book. The radio station offered to sell me airtime to promote the practice. While professional salespeople were trying to close sales with me, I waited patiently for patients. All I wanted to do was practice my profession and help animals. Plenty of people wanted to help me spend money. First, I needed to make some.

With college loans to pay off and drug inventory to purchase, I had no money to spend on advertising. I decided that instead of focusing on closing sales to farmers and pet owners, I would work on opening relationships with people. During my entire career, I have found that relationships do more to stimulate business than any form of paid advertising. It may be easier to buy an ad than to create a friendship, but investments in relationships will always produce the greatest rewards—financial, social, and personal.

> *Advertising will help get people in the door of a business, but what happens after that is dependent upon relationships.*

Because everyone in the area knew everyone else, referrals from clients built my early dairy farm practice. The Bender brothers, Plagenzs, Jahnkes, and Lapers were all related through marriages. The Dornfeld, Floeter, Damerow, Siewert, Schultz, Drews, and Grams farms were distant neighbors. The Schwandt, Fox, and Nowatski farms were close to the clinic. Roger Schure and Ken Dahlke farmed near each other and bowled together with many other clients. The Eberts, Mielkes, Kelms, and Millers became more than just business relationships. My best clients were also my best friends. Relationships with farmers were essential to my business; they became my social life as well.

❖ "Friendship with oneself is all-important, because without it one cannot be friends with anyone else."

—Eleanor Roosevelt

A key factor in creating and continuing success in business is building solid relationships with current clients and customers. It is more expensive to find new clients than it is to work harder and do more for present clientele. In my practice we treat animals with drugs, medications, and surgery. We treat people with respect, courtesy, kindness, and consideration. We advertise very little as our marketing plan still relies upon referrals to keep our business strong.

The relationships and bonds people create with animals can be as strong as any between humans. Some people get along better with pets than with people. Dogs and cats replace kids in many families, either as child substitutes or to fill empty nests when the children have left home. It is not uncommon for veterinarians to hear an adult child say, "I wish my parents treated me as well when I was a kid as they do their dog today." One of my favorite lines came from a young lady in her thirties who had a very strong bond with her pet. She said, "I came close to marriage several times, but the boys I met didn't get along with my cat. When a guy would say, 'Either the cat goes or I do,' it was a no-brainer decision for me."

Recently, I referred a very old pet to a veterinary internal medicine specialist because it had a serious health problem. A few years ago I would have said it had a terminal illness, but with advancements in technology, pharmacology, and surgical skills, treatment was now a possibility. After a thorough examination, the doctor told the owners that they had a fairly good chance of saving the dog. To make sure that my clients wanted to make an investment in the dog that might exceed $5,000, she asked, "Are you sure you want this dog? There are many others in animal shelters and pet shops that are looking for good homes." My clients assured the referring doctor that they had the money and would do whatever possible to keep their pet alive. The relationship they had with their pet was more important than any financial consideration.

The other option for the owners was to put their pet to sleep. When I have to perform euthanasia, I am often asked if pets go to heaven. I tell people that the life-force in a beloved pet will always be a part of their heart. There is no question about eternal life from my perspective, for ani-

❧ "Nothing is a greater impediment to being on good terms with others than being ill at ease with yourself."

—Honore de Balzac

mals or people. You may not always be able to play "fetch" with your dog or curl up with your kitty, but you will always be able to connect with them through your thoughts. When an animal is a part of your life, the relationship is eternal.

Relationships are essential in human medicine as well. Selecting a personal physician may not be a business decision for you, but it is the doctor's business. Perhaps you chose a doctor because of location, the limitations of your HMO or insurance plan, or because someone told you about the physician. Once you visit a doctor, return visits are based more on your relationship with the physician, nurse, and receptionist than on any other factor. Granted there are times you don't get to select a physician, but when you can, chances are you choose a knowledgeable doctor with whom you can establish rapport and build an ongoing relationship.

What are business relationships worth? If you are in business for the long haul, relationships are priceless. Business executive Harvey Mackay, author of *Swim With the Sharks Without Being Eaten Alive*, is an expert on building business relationships. He suggests we do more than just collect names of people when we build a network of relationships. His contact file includes a person's address, title or position at work, company name or organization, birthday and place of birth, connections and times of past meetings, family details that are important to the individual, educational background, affiliations with organizations, civic and religious groups, special interests, career history, accomplishments, and more.

> "*The ability to deal with people is as purchasable a commodity as sugar and coffee. And I will pay more for that ability than for any other under the sun.*"
> —*John D. Rockefeller* ☙

You can buy a Rolodex® just like Mackay's and fill it with just as many business cards. But I'll bet you Mr. Mackay would not trade his Rolodex® for yours even if you threw in $10,000 to boot. It is not about the tool or the paper or the ink on the cards. The value of his Rolodex® is in the relationships he has created with the individuals in the file. In another of Mackay's

❧ "If you make friends with yourself, you will never be alone."

—Anon.

202

books, *The Harvey Mackay Rolodex® Network Builder,* he warrants his system of creating business relationships. "It is one of the few tools that's absolutely, positively guaranteed to work."

Whatever it is you do in life to earn a living, you will be successful to the degree that you build relationships with other people. Relationships are critical in businesses that sell goods or services and are built on trust, confidence, and friendships. Teamwork, employee retention, customer relations, and increased sales are all a result of developing solid relationships. By building relationships we can obtain all the physical things we need or want.

> "*Prosperity should come to us not at the expense of our friendships, but by the expanse of our relationships.*"
>
> —*Vetdini* ❧

> *Customers make purchases based on emotions and then justify their decisions with facts.*

Relationships and conflict

People join together in times of crisis. Spouses argue and bicker in their own homes yet defend one another in the presence of strangers. Children fight with siblings within the family but join together to fight with rival gangs. Cities and counties who dispute tax revenues from the state band together as a state to dispute tax revenues from the national government. States that battle trade laws and federal mandates unite as a country in fighting foreign wars. The nations of the world would likely join forces to battle invaders from other planets. Conflict draws people together. It is peace that challenges relationships.

When the people in a family or a state must combine forces to survive, camaraderie is natural and develops spontaneously. When there is peace and no need to unite, that is when you must work at strengthening relationships by putting energy into your friendships. Friendships build stronger families, communities, and nations. Woodrow Wilson said, "Friendship is the only cement that will ever hold the world together."

❧ "I have friends in overalls whose friendship I would not swap for the favor of the kings of the world."

—Thomas A. Edison

> "*If two friends ask you to judge a dispute, don't accept, because you will lose one friend; on the other hand, if two strangers come with the same request, accept, because you will gain one.*"
>
> —St. Augustine

While listening to public radio, I heard a proponent of peace relate her fears of global annihilation. She said that at any minute a nuclear war could start a chain reaction that would destroy every living creature on the planet. She went on to state how many trillions of dollars the U.S. spends on military actions and defense systems. Then she said something that really caught my attention. She claimed that if we had all of the money spent on war in the last ten years we could use it to solve all the problems of the world. Her statement nullified any respect or empathy I might have had for her cause. While I agree that war wastes lives, money, and resources—war never determines who is right, only who is left—I passionately disagree with her premise that money fixes problems. The reason we have war and starvation and other problems is not lack of money. It is more likely lust for money. It is my biased opinion that conflicts in relationships cause most of the world's problems, which could be resolved if the rich and powerful shared more with the poor and weak.

Most psychotherapy has to do with relationships, and relationship counseling is a thriving business. Psychiatrists, psychologists, social workers, psychotherapists, ministers, priests, and rabbis function as mental health providers to resolve conflict within relationships. They counsel:

- parents with children,
- grandparents with grandchildren,
- teachers with students,
- employees with employers,
- spouses with spouses,
- spouses with lovers,
- victims with assailants,
- and even people with themselves.

Once we are able to resolve conflict between individuals, we will do a much better job of resolving conflict between countries.

> *While exercise and diet are essential to a healthy and happy life, neither will keep you fit without good relationships.*

SMARTER Success is not about how to create and enjoy lasting relationships. There are literally thousand of books that purport to do just that. In a recent search for books on relationships, one Internet bookseller listed almost 32,000 titles. Libraries have many more. There are books about all sorts of relationships, including:

- Couples—dating, courtship, pre-marriage, marriage, divorce, romance, quarreling fair.
- Parenting—children getting along with children, dealing with daughters, handling sons, interacting with daycare providers and teachers.
- Friendships—making friends, keeping friends, dumping friends.

There were 650 books specific to business relationships:

- Employee relationships—management, labor, team building, interpersonal.
- Trade relationships—selling, marketing, brand loyalty.
- Customer/client relationships—satisfaction, conflict resolution.
- Community relationships—foundations, civic group support.

SMARTER Success is about the importance of relationships. Setting a goal to *be* something can build relationships by planning to create and nurture them from the beginning. Setting a goal to *have* something can break down relationships by neglecting, ignoring, or dissolving them. When you use the *SMARTER Success* system and strive to build relationships, you naturally create health, happiness, peace, and prosperity.

The story of the Babson brothers ties these ideas together and illustrates the importance of relationships as we reach for goals. John and Greg Babson were twins who loved animals and were destined to become veterinarians. The boys had an ongoing argument about who was born first, who was more intelligent, more athletic, and better looking, but for the most part they were very similar kids. Both brothers went to the same university and graduated from veterinary school in the same class. As veterinarians, they found jobs in separate cities 150 miles apart, but both chose to practice on pets. They both married, but their lives drifted in different directions. As adults, they never had as much in common as they did when they were kids, that is, until they lost their houses on the same day, shortly after their thirty-fifth birthdays.

John was the more aggressive of the two boys. He joined a large practice in a huge animal hospital. There were six other veterinarians, twelve veterinary technicians, three receptionists, and many other part-time helpers. The group practice offered the very best care possible and featured some of the latest technology for diagnosing and treating pet problems. John was compensated with a sizable salary and fantastic benefits. If he stayed on with the clinic and treated his quota of patients every day, he would be able to climb the corporate ladder within the practice and someday become a co-owner.

Within months of starting at the clinic, John had so many clients he couldn't remember their names. He avoided eye contact when he met people in public, which made him appear haughty and aloof. He was actually a very caring and compassionate person with a lot on his mind.

John married Kristi, a girl he had met in college, and together they had three children, two boys and a girl. Kristi was John's princess and he treated her well. She had a credit card and loved to go shopping for clothes and things for the house. She loved to host elaborate cocktail parties and dinners for their many friends. John often sent her flowers, and when he wasn't too busy they would go out to late-night dinners together. Kristi seemed to be a very happy homemaker.

John was a great father and provider. The kids achieved good grades in school and when they needed help, tutors came to the house. The children always wore the latest fashions, name brand shoes, and designer label clothes. They had the coolest bicycles, roller blades, and computer games. All three children took piano, voice, and dance lessons at one time or another. Mom videotaped performances for Dad who was always too busy at the clinic to attend. John sponsored a soccer team for the kids and did make it to the end of several games each summer. Once he even hired a limousine to haul the lucky kids to a game when it was his turn to carpool.

The children were provided with a good religious education. Every Sunday morning John dropped the children off at the church. He also supported the church school building fund by donating over $3,000 each year. After John unloaded the kids, he drove his Porsche to the country club. John liked to golf and spent much of his free time on the links. He had a regular foursome with whom he could talk about the stock market, business, and things the men had in common.

The whole family went on a two-week vacation every year. Disney World was their favorite destination. John bought an eighteen-foot ski boat which they used at least twice each summer. During the holiday season they got together in alternating years with Kristi's parents or John's. The family appeared to enjoy being together.

Greg was more laid back than John. He joined a much smaller practice with an older veterinarian, and the two of them had a simple mission statement for their clinic: "To help people with their pets." They were more interested in making friends than money. Greg quickly learned the names of most of the clients and knew them well.

Greg married Gail, a girl who grew up not far from the clinic. Together they also had three children, two girls and a boy in between. Their social life revolved around their family. When they met with friends, the children were always included. Gail and Greg had a regular date night when the two of them went to a restaurant just to be alone together. The family went camping on weekends, visited the in-laws often, and attended church together on Sundays. Greg donated two hours a week to church committee work, and Gail helped organize and run the church youth group.

The children had nice clothes and toys, but not designer or expensive. They did well in school because Greg and Gail insisted that homework be done before the family dinner each evening. If they needed help, either Greg or Gail was there to offer assistance and guidance. The kids played sports and Greg managed a team and attended most games. Gail and Greg took turns with car pools, and together they watched piano and dance recitals year after year.

Greg and John lived twin lives up until they began their professional careers. As children they were similar. As veterinarians, husbands, and fathers they were quite different from each other. John pursued goals to have a large practice and to provide luxuries for his wife and children. Greg invested his time in creating relationships with his clients as well as his family. As adults, their lives were unique, until they both lost their houses.

Greg could see the smoke billowing high up into the sky as he drove home for lunch. As he turned the corner onto his street, he could see that it was his house which was in flames. His hysterical wife and their three screaming kids were across the street. Together, the family watched the firefighters do all they could to save the house, but it was hopeless. The house and everything in it was lost. Later, it was discovered that the fire started with the combustion of some paint rags in the basement utility storeroom.

The very same day, John came home late in the evening after work to find his house intact, but no one at home. A note from his wife was on the kitchen table. "Dear John, Where have you been? The kids and I hardly know you anymore. We've gone to Mom's for a week. That should be enough time for you to get all of your belongings out of the house. I want a divorce. You can have your clinic, car, and country club. I'm taking the house and the children."

Greg lost his house because he had not been paying attention to the relationship between the flammable fumes of paint rags and the open flame of the basement water heater.

John lost his house because he had not been paying attention to the relationships between the family (his) and the father (himself!). He had been too busy creating money in his business to develop meaning in his relationships.

Both brothers created goals to *have* things and goals to *be* things, but John assigned priority to *having* a large income, a wife, children, a house, a car, a boat, and a lot of friends. He established and sustained his relationships with money and the things money can buy.

Greg concentrated on *being* a husband, a father, a friend, a doctor for pets, and a provider of necessities for his family. His life emphasized relationships with his family, his friends, his clients, and his God.

The Babson brothers are typical examples of similar people who have dissimilar goals and priorities. It really doesn't matter if you actually use the SMART or SMARTER techniques to set your goals. What matters is how you think about a goal, what you pursue as a goal, and how you pursue it. The two systems both work, but they can produce significantly different results. If you believe relationships are important, consider setting and pursuing SMARTER goals.

> *SMARTER goals create longevity. Relationships built while pursuing being goals continue long after relationships with material things expire.*

Those who are truly successful know that SMARTER goals are relationship building.

Epilogue

Smart, Smarter, Smartest

Somewhere along the way, you need to find your own path to peace and prosperity, if that is how you define success. Whether or not you become successful, or rather, whether or not you believe you *are* successful, is really up to you. Whatever technique you use to pursue your goals, or if you use no methodology at all, your success is dependent upon your own perception of your condition.

Perhaps you have accepted a version of the established SMART technique as a logical, efficient way to set and attain goals when you want to *have* something. Maybe you have used the technique because you heard about SMART from someone you regard as successful, someone you look up to, or someone who has great authority, influence, and charisma.

> It is wise to imitate your mentors, but don't be intimidated by those who claim to be successful and then say that you must become successful their way. What works for someone else may not work for you.

Now you also know about the SMARTER technique for setting goals. You heard about it from an animal doctor as a natural way to *be* successful, happy, and healthy. As with any system, it has room for improvement; it can and should be altered or customized if it is to work for you. Think about it when you consider what you want for your future, especially if you set a goal to *be* something.

There are undoubtedly many other types of goals and different systems, acrostics, acronyms, methods, and schemes that can help you establish goals. Somewhere along the way, someone might suggest a SMARTEST way to set goals and claim it is the best. If it were indeed the best and smartest way to set a goal, then it would be the ultimate technique. The SMARTEST system would replace all the others and everyone could set goals the same way for the same things.

But that would be ridiculous and unrealistic. We don't all think the same way. We will never want to pursue exactly the same dreams. We have different goals and should have different ways of reaching for them. Success is a do-it-yourself project and should be approached in a do-it-unique way.

The 4-H club to which I belonged as a youth—an organization I still support as an adult—has a motto: "To make the best better." The group recognizes the possibility that whatever can be created can be improved. Good is acceptable, best is the ultimate, but we should try to make the best even better. The 4-H motto inspired me to think about a SMARTER technique for setting goals and ignore the potential of a SMARTEST technique.

The superlative form of any adjective referring to human performance should be used only when the comparative form is impossible. The words *smartest* and *best* imply that there is no possibility of improvement, which is very unlikely. The only time there is no room for improvement is when you quit trying. Even at the top there is more space above to reach higher. The inspirational speaker Les Brown once said, "If improvement is possible, then excellent is not good enough." To be excellent, to be your best, or to set a SMARTEST goal implies an end point beyond which you cannot improve. That only happens if you give up.

> *If SMARTER is possible, SMARTEST is not good enough.*

People often ask me, "Do you really believe the stuff you write? Does life really work that way? Do you personally use goals to obtain and become everything you desire?" Years ago when I started working on this book, I was unsure of the answers to those questions. Today, I can answer them all with certainty. I do believe, or rather, I *know* that life does provide me with everything I need to fulfill my every desire, as long as what I wish for is meant to be. This isn't to say that I wait for things to happen and then decide that is what I wanted to have happen. But if things don't work out the way I wish, I can accept the outcome as the way things should be. Art Linkletter taught me, "Things work out best for those who make the best out of the way things work out." His idea works better than complaining about or trying to change what happened in the past.

To me, success cannot be measured by the accumulation of material possessions. Success in life is not a big home, a summer cottage, a new car, jewelry, or gems. I truly believe my value in this world is measured by how much I would be worth if I lost all of my money. The greatest success in life comes from the recognition and appreciation of the world's abundance, not the accumulation of it. The greatest treasures we cannot own. Priceless possessions are free. Wealth exists in the minds of those who sustain the proper thoughts. Success means living with peace of mind in a state of health and happiness.

To know how to *be* happy and healthy while exploring your personal path is a simple goal worthy of whatever effort it takes. A journey through life is made meaningful when it benefits others. Life is more peaceful when you live it balanced in timeless harmony with everything around you. Relationships built along the way become even more valuable when you realize that nothing is worthwhile without the love and respect of others.

You will *have* everything you need when you become the person you are meant to *be*.

Somewhere along the way,

    SMARTER *Success*

        can help you *be* successful

            in your own world,

                at your own pace,

                    and in your own way.

One of the challenges in life is to find your path and then maintain your direction. Your course will need adjustments, perhaps constant corrections as you pursue your goals and interact with the desires of those around you. It is natural to forget what you have learned and know to be true, so refer to this text when your life becomes too complicated, appears meaningless, out of balance, your emotions rule or when your relationships change or create conflict.

Notes about quotes

People generally accept ideas much more readily when they are told someone famous, perhaps Benjamin Franklin, said the words first. Therefore, quotations of famous people have been inserted into this text at appropriate points to lend credibility.

The quotations cited throughout this book are as accurate as possible at the time of production. Some sources used for research and verification cite speakers who actually repeated what someone else had already said. It is sometimes impossible to determine who uttered a phrase first. Some of the selections undoubtedly have been embellished through time as the originators gained fame. Also, it is interesting that most of the old quotations are attributed to men. Quotations of women who lived hundreds of years ago are hard to find. In my estimation, the credit for many truisms should not go to men, but rather to their mothers and wives who are likely responsible for creating many of the best maxims.

Some of the aphorisms have no credits listed because they were misplaced or have multiple etiologies. Perhaps you recognize the origin. Maybe you said it first. This author has constructed some of the sayings. With apologies and gratitude extended to those who claim credit for any unique arrangements of words, the ideas herein are offered to help you realize your own path to success.

SMARTER *Success* contains quotations and mentions of more than a hundred significant people. While you know many of them, some may be unfamiliar. Presented here in alphabetical order is a little information about them and the dates of their births and deaths if they have passed on. What they said and did between those dates created lasting legacies for past, present, and future generations.

John Quincy Adams (1767–1848), sixth President of the United Sates, diplomat, legislator

James Lane Allen (1849–1925), writer, educator

Woody Allen (1935–present), American actor, writer, filmmaker

Greg Anderson (?–present), author of *The 22 Non-Negotiable Laws of Wellness*

St. Augustine (354–430), Church father, philosopher

St. Francis of Assisi (1182?–1226), Italian monk, founder of Franciscan order

St. Thomas Aquinas (1225?–1274), Italian theologian, philosopher

Aristotle (384–322 B.C.), Greek philosopher

Marcus Aurelius (121–180), Emperor of Rome from 161 until his death

Honore de Balzac (1799–1850), French author

Henry Ward Beecher (1813–1887), American clergyman, editor, abolitionist

John Belushi (1949–1982), comedian, actor

Black Elk (1863–1950), native American religious leader

Erma Bombeck (1927–1996), American author, humorist

Buddha (563?–483? B.C.), Indian philosopher, founder of Buddhism

Robert Browning (1812–1889), English poet

Warren Buffett (1930–present), American financial wizard

Eric Butterworth (1916–2003), popular Unity minister, author

Leo Buscaglia (1924–1998), self–help guru

Dale Carnegie (1888–1955), American author, educator

Miguel de Cervantes (1547–1616), Spanish author

Paul Cezanne (1839–1906), French cubist and abstract painter

Jennie Jerome Churchill (1854–1921), mother of Winston Churchill

Winston Churchill (1874–1965), English prime minister, Nobel prize 1953

Cicero (106–43 B.C.), Roman statesman, orator, philosopher

Steve Clark (1960–1991), member of band Def Leppard

George S. Clason (1926–?), Author of *The Richest Man in Babylon*.

Kurt Cobain (1967–1994), member of band Nirvana

Calvin Coolidge (1872–1933), thirtieth U.S. President

Norman Cousins (1915–1980), American editor, writer

Charles Darwin (1809–1882), English naturalist

Emily Dickinson (1830–1886), American poet

Everett M. Dirksen (1896–1969), American legislator

Benjamin Disraeli (1804–1881), British prime minister, author, diplomat

George Eastman (1854–1932), American inventor, industrialist, philanthropist

Albert Einstein (1879–1955), German–born American theoretical physicist Nobel prize 1921

George Eliot (1819–1880), English novelist

Ralph Waldo Emerson (1803–1882), American poet, essayist

Epictetus (first or second century A.D.), Greek stoic philosopher

Epicurus (342–270), Greek philosopher

Sally Field (1946–present), television and movie actress

Henry Ford (1863–1947), American automobile manufacturer

Anne Frank (1929–1945), Dutch Jewish diarist

Viktor Frankl (1905–1997), psychologist, philosopher, survivor of WWII concentration camp

Benjamin Franklin (1706–1790), American statesman, diplomat, scientist, printer

Thomas Fuller (1608–1661), English clergyman

Mahatma Gandhi (1869–1948), Indian nationalist and spiritual leader

Bill Gates (1955–present), founder of Microsoft

Kahlil Gibran (1883–1931), Syrian–born American mystic, poet, painter

Rob Gilbert Ph.D., (?), editor, *Bits & Pieces*

Giorgione (1478?–1510), Italian painter of non–religious subjects

Horace Greeley (1811–1872), American journalist and politician

Johann von Goethe (1749–1832), German author

Pete Ham (1947–1975), member of band Badfinger

Dag Hammarskjold (1905–1961), Swedish statesman, Secretary–General of the United Nations

Jimi Hendrix (1942–1970), guitar master

Conrad Hilton (1887–1979), American businessman, founder of Hilton Hotels

Adolph Hitler (1889–1945), Austrian–born German Nazi dictator

Oliver Wendell Holmes, Jr (1841–1935), American jurist

Elias Howe (1819–1867), American inventor and manufacturer

Aldous Leonard Huxley (1894–963), English author

William James (1842–1910), American psychologist and philosopher

Thomas Jefferson (1743–1826), third U.S. President, author, scientist, architect, educator, diplomat

Karen Johnson (?–present), registered nurse, philanthropist

Janis Joplin (1940–1970), singer

Carl Jung (1875–1961), Swiss psychologist and psychiatrist

Helen Keller (1880–1968), blind/deaf author, lecturer)

Father James Keller (1900–1977), founder of The Christophers

Martin Luther King, Jr. (1929–1968), American clergyman, civil–rights leader, Nobel prize 1964

Leonardo da Vinci (1452–1519), artist, engineer, musician, scientist

Abraham Lincoln (1809–1865), sixteenth U.S. president

Linie (1998–present), golden retriever

Henry Wadsworth Longfellow (1807–1882), American poet

Harvey Mackay (?–present), business executive, author

Maxwell Maltz, M.D. (~1899–1975) facial surgeon, author, motivational speaker

Og Mandino (1923–1996), writer, philosopher

Pierre Carlet de Chamblain de Marivaux (1688–1763), French author

Abraham Maslow (1908–1970), psychologist

Herman Melville (1819–1891), American author

Bobby McFerrin (1950–present), singer

David O. McKay (1873–1970), Church of Latter–day Saints

William Menninger (1899–1966), psychiatrist

Marilyn Monroe (1926–1962), actor, movie star

Christopher Morley (1890–1957), American novelist, journalist

Jim Morrison (1943–1971), member of band The Doors

Bob Nelson (?–present), author of *1001 Ways to Reward Employees* ISBN 1–56305–339–X

Earl Nightingale (1933–1989), radio personality, motivational speaker

Ovid (43 B.C.–A.D. 18), Roman poet

John Panozzo (1948–1996), member of band Styx

Norman Vincent Peale (1898–1993), American clergyman and author

James Cash Penney (1875–1971), American businessman, founder of department store

Mary Pickford (1893–1979), Canadian–born American actress

Titus Maccius Plautus (254?–184 B.C.), Roman playwright

Edgar Allan Poe (1809–1849), American author

Colin Powell (1937–present), U.S. General, U.S. Secretary of State

Elvis Presley (1935–1977), singer, "King" of rock & roll

Freddie Prinze (1954–1977), television actor

Rainer Maria Rilke (1875–1926), German–Austrian lyric poet

John D. Rockefeller (1839–1937), Philanthropist

Will Rogers (1879–1935), American author, actor

Jim Rohn (?–present), business philosopher, speaker, author

Eleanor Roosevelt (1884–1962), American diplomat, author, political figure, wife of FDR

Franklin Delano Roosevelt (1882–1945), thirty–second U.S. President

Theodore Roosevelt (1858–1919), twenty–sixth U.S. President

Anwar Sadat (1918–1981), Egyptian statesman

George Sand (1804–1876), French Novelist

Albert Schweitzer (1875–1965), French philosopher, physician, musician, Nobel 1952

Bon Scott (1946–1980), member of band AC/DC

William Shakespeare (1564–1616), English playwright and poet

Bernie S. Siegel, MD (?–present), American surgeon and author

Aleksander Solzhenitsyn (1918–present), Russian author, Nobel 1970

Robert Louis Stevenson (1850–1894), Scottish poet and novelist

Vinnie Taylor (1949–1974), member of band Sha Na Na

Margaret Thatcher (1925–present), British prime minister

Mother Teresa (1910–1997), Albanian–born Indian nun, Nobel 1979

Henry David Thoreau (1817–1862), American essayist, naturalist, poet

Leo Tolstoy (1828–1910), Russian author, philosopher

Brian Tracy (1944–present), speaker, author, business consultant

Mark Twain pen name of Samuel Longhorne Clemens (1835–1910), American author, humorist

Vincent Van Gogh (1853–1890), Dutch painter who produced ~800 oil paintings, sold one

Vetdini pseudonym of Dr. Alan Lippart (1952–present), veterinarian, educator

Sid Vicious (1957–1979), musician in band Sex Pistols

Booker T. Washington (1856–1915), Educator, author

Martha Washington (1731–1802), wife of George Washington, 1st U.S. President

Marianne Williamson (?–present), *A Course in Miracles* leader, spiritual lecturer

Woodrow T. Wilson (1856–1924), twenty–eighth U.S. President, educator, author

Oprah Winfrey (1954–present), television personality

John Wooden (1910–present), UCLA basketball coach

William Wordsworth (1770–1850), British poet

Frank Lloyd Wright (1869–1959), American architect

Zig Zigler (?–present), salesman, speaker, author

Give the gift of SMARTER Success

Give the gift of knowledge and give a copy of *SMARTER Success* for graduations, birthdays, weddings, or holidays. *SMARTER Success* is the perfect present for the person who seems to have everything.

> Inspire those you care about to find their own paths to health, happiness, peace, and prosperity by reaching for SMARTER goals.

Order your additional copies of *SMARTER Success* at www.smartersuccess.com or at your favorite booksore. You can also order this book by contacting the publisher at:

MVC Productions
P.O. Box 614
Markesan, WI 53946

To learn more...

For more information about *SMARTER Success* seminars, keynotes, and consultations, visit www.Lippart.com or contact the author at:

Dr. Al Lippart
P.O. Box 614
Markesan, WI 53946

For copies of Sarah Riley's illustrations, request a free brochure catalog of her work by writing to:

Art@SmarterSuccess.com